Quakers
and the
Atlantic Culture

QUAKERS
AND THE
ATLANTIC CULTURE

by
Frederick B. Tolles

New York THE MACMILLAN COMPANY 1960

The Macmillan Company, New York
Brett-Macmillan Ltd., Galt, Ontario

Library of Congress catalog card number: 60–7085

TO THE MEMORY OF

My Mother

who, as the Maine lobsterman said,
had "good courage"

Foreword

It is possible to write a book in installments over a period of fifteen years without realizing it—without realizing, that is, that it is actually a book one is writing. Yet if a scholar has concerned himself fairly steadily over a period of years with a single problem or a group of closely related problems, it will not be too surprising if the essays in which from time to time he sets down his findings form a coherent whole—in fact, a book. That is what the author of these essays discovered when a period of illness in the summer of 1958 prevented him from doing any further research and writing and gave him an opportunity to review the product of the previous decade and a half.

1

The central problem with which I had concerned myself was the relationship of the Society of Friends to its social and intellectual environment. Though the Society of Friends is and always has been a relatively small religious body, I do not regard Quaker history as a narrow subject. In fact, part of my concern has been to enlarge its boundaries to their proper dimensions. Too often in the past it has been conceived as denominational annals, directed primarily to a limited audience of Friends, and restricted largely to the internal development of the Society, without much regard to the interplay between the small world of Quakerdom and the great world beyond its borders. By contrast I have chosen to consider the subject in the broadest possible context—as a phase of the ancient and nearly universal problem of the church and the world, of Christianity and civilization, or, as H. Richard Niebuhr calls it, of "Christ and culture."

A brief reference to Professor Niebuhr's brilliant analysis of the possible relationships between a religious group and its culture will suggest the complexity of the subject. If one thinks, for example, of the Quakers' rejection of war and their sense of being a "peculiar people" set off from the world, one might be inclined to align the Society of Friends with those who have found it a religious duty to reject their culture and renounce its values. But Niebuhr quite rightly observes that the Friends as a body have represented this attitude ("Christ *against* culture") less consistently than, say, the Mennonites. He submits—and there is much evidence for it—that many modern Quakers, especially in the liberal wing of the Society, show a greater affinity to the opposite attitude ("the Christ *of* culture"), that they have tended to identify the Christian teaching with their own "finest ideals, their noblest institutions, and their best philosophy."[1] But one can readily find in Quaker history many examples of the other typical attitudes which Niebuhr distinguishes ("Christ *above* culture," "Christ and culture *in paradox*," "Christ *the transformer of* culture"), all of which in one way or another contrive to accept the claims of both Christianity and civilization, while recognizing that at many crucial points they are in opposition to each other.

My primary concern, however, has not been to identify and catalogue these attitudes in Quakerism, for my approach is not, like Niebuhr's, typological and analytical, but historical. I am content to show how different attitudes toward culture have prevailed at different periods of Quaker history and in different sectors of the Society of Friends. Another way of stating my purpose would be to say that I have tried to demonstrate the difficulty of making simple generalizations about Friends over the three centuries of their history. Or, to put it in still another way, to show that the Religious Society of Friends, like any other human organization, has been subject to historical and cultural change, at the same time that it has been in certain realms the initiator of change.

This is not to suggest that the Inward Light, the source of guidance to which the Friends have always looked, is a will-o'-the-wisp, leading now this way, now that, in response to cultural conditioning. It is rather to point out that Quaker history is, after all, part of history, that the Spirit, which "bloweth where it listeth," has led its followers to respond in differing ways to the challenges of successive eras and, equally, that the "Children of the Light" have also been children of their times, and therefore imperfect receivers and transmitters of the divine message.

Though I trust I have collected and presented the historical evidence honestly, as becomes a historian, I have not tried to conceal my Quaker bias in interpreting it. I am a member of the Society of Friends, and deeply committed (though inadequately obedient) to its religious teachings. At the same time I hope I have not been uncritical. Dr. Johnson once confessed that he liked the "encomiastic parts" of history best, but I think Friends have had more than enough of panegyric from the pens of starry-eyed admirers. What is needed— I think most Friends will agree—is *critical* history that will weigh and measure all our mistakes and shortcomings—and there have been bushels of them. To weigh and measure, after all, is the proper function of a bushel, but we are nowhere commanded to use this utensil for the concealment of light. And so in the brief introductions which precede the essays and seek to relate them to one another, I have ventured to suggest ways in which past Quaker insights into Truth might speak to some of the problems of the modern world. For assuredly modern man needs every gleam of light that gives any promise of leading him out of the dark wilderness of contemporary culture.

One responsibility I have shamefully shirked. Though I have used the terms "culture" and "civilization" frequently, I have not attempted to define them or to distinguish between them. That task I leave to the anthropologists, who are doing it all the time. I have assumed that the reader has his own understanding of these vague but essential concepts and that it does not differ greatly from mine. Nor have I felt it necessary to deal comprehensively with every segment of culture. No doubt if I were writing this book *de novo*, it would assume a somewhat different shape. Probably I should choose to alter some of the emphases; possibly I should include additional facets of culture to which Quakerism has stood in a significant relationship. Nevertheless, I send this book forth with no more than an author's usual misgivings, conscious that the more obvious portions of the story—the Quaker impulse to humanitarian activity, for example, or the Quaker criticism of war—have been treated by others, and hopeful that where there are serious omissions, as there unquestionably are, someone will be stimulated to make them good, and thus to fill out our knowledge of the Quaker contribution to our culture.

The two opening chapters are designed to set Quakerism, especially early American Quakerism, in its cultural matrix, the North Atlantic world, and to anatomize the remarkable transoceanic community which the early Friends created. After a half-century of looking westward and concentrating on the unique, the native, the distinctively American features of American history—the consequence of Frederick Jackson Turner's momentous discovery of the frontier—American historians are now looking eastward again and acknowledging that our culture from the beginning has been part of what Professor Michael Kraus calls "the Atlantic civilization." And no religious group, says Professor Kraus, "had closer transatlantic ties than did the Quakers."² Such was the cultural homogeneity of English and American Quakerism, at least down to the end of the eighteenth century, that I have felt justified throughout these essays in writing of the Society of Friends as one community, and have drawn material indiscriminately from the writings and records of Friends in the British Isles and the American colonies. I don't know whether the term "Atlantic culture," which I have used in my title, is yet an expression in common use or not. But if it is not, it should be. For it seems to me as useful and necessary a term as the indispensable phrase "Mediterranean culture," which we use to denominate the civilization of the ancient world.

In Chapter III I discuss the attitudes of English and American Quakers toward politics, showing how they have swung back and forth, pendulum-fashion, now toward wholehearted participation as a religious duty, now toward complete abstention for fear of compromising Quaker ideals.

No one would deny that capitalism, or "free enterprise," and experimental science have been two of the major shaping forces in modern Western culture. Recent investigations in historical sociology, elaborating the seminal insights of Max Weber, have stressed the role of the "Protestant ethic," and particularly the ethic of Puritanism, broadly conceived, in preparing the ground for the growth of these momentous phenomena. In Chapter IV I attempt to isolate the elements in early Quaker thought and practice which played creatively into the development of these ideologies.

Chapter V deals with Quakerism and the arts—an unpromising topic at first glance, but one which clearly reveals the tensions and changes in Quaker attitudes toward the "world" and its culture.

I have included an essay on the reaction of the Philadelphia Friends to the Great Awakening, America's first outburst of revivalism in religion (Chapter VI), for a number of reasons. Revivalism has unquestionably been a characteristic element of American culture. The Quaker response to it in the 1740's not only tells us something about the character of eighteenth century urban Quakerism and how far it had accommodated itself to upper-class culture, but something too about the nature of religious "enthusiasm" and the way in which Philadelphia Friends had outgrown it.[3]

The final chapter is an attempt to place the Quaker culture in relation to the other ways of life that flourished in early Pennsylvania, America's first experiment in cultural pluralism.

If there are any peculiar twists to my reading of early Quaker history, they are undoubtedly these three, none of them particularly original: an acceptance of the English and Puritan as opposed to the Continental and mystical origins of the Quaker movement; an emphasis on the corporate rather than on the individualistic character of Quaker religious experience; and a disposition to regard primitive Quakerism as primarily a form of enthusiastic, or prophetic, rather than mystical religion. At these points my interpretation diverges from the views commonly held over the past three or four decades— views largely shaped by the historical writings of Rufus M. Jones. I wish here to pay my tribute to the luminous scholarship of that greatest of modern Quakers, while demonstrating, I hope, that the history of Quakerism, like the history of anything worth studying, can be fully understood only if it is studied in relation to all the elements— social, political, economic, intellectual, artistic—that make up the rich design of Clio's garment. It is my hope that the essays which compose this volume are written in this spirit.

2

"The Atlantic Community of the Early Friends" was written as a Presidential Address to the Friends' Historical Society, and delivered before the Society in Lancaster, England, in 1952; it was

originally printed as Supplement No. 24 to the *Journal of the Friends'
Historical Society* (London, 1952). "The Transatlantic Quaker Community in the Seventeenth Century: Its Structure and Functioning"
was read at a meeting of the American Historical Association in Chicago in 1950 and published under the title "The Transatlantic Quaker
Community in the Seventeenth Century" in the *Huntington Library
Quarterly*, XIV (1951), 239–258. "Quakerism and Politics" was the
1956 Ward Lecture at Guilford College and was separately printed
by the college. "Quakerism, Capitalism, and Science" is made up of
two short essays first published independently: "Benjamin Franklin's
Business Mentors: The Philadelphia Quaker Merchants," which was
first read at a meeting of the Pennsylvania Historical Association in
1946 and printed in the *William and Mary Quarterly*, 3rd Series, IV
(1947), 60–69; and "Quakerism and the 'New Philosophy,'" which
originally appeared as part of Chapter 9 (pp. 205–213) of *Meeting
House and Counting House: The Quaker Merchants of Colonial
Philadelphia* (Chapel Hill, N.C., 1948). "The Quaker Esthetic" was
originally delivered as a lecture at the University of Delaware and
later published in the *American Quarterly*, XI (1959) 484–501. "Quietism Versus Enthusiasm: The Philadelphia Quakers and the Great
Awakening" appeared in the *Pennsylvania Magazine of History and
Biography*, LXIX (1945), 26–49. "The Culture of Early Pennsylvania"
was originally a lecture delivered at Bryn Mawr College at a symposium on early Pennsylvania history in 1956; it was printed in the
Pennsylvania Magazine of History and Biography, LXXXI (1957),
119–137.

The articles which originally appeared in periodicals are reprinted
here with the kind permission of the editors of the several journals.
"Quakerism and Politics" is reproduced with the permission of the
President of Guilford College. "Quakerism and the 'New Philos-
ophy'" is reprinted by permission of the University of North Carolina
Press.

In several minor respects the articles have been revised. Remarks
appropriate only to the circumstances of oral delivery have been removed. In most of the instances where I had used the same quotation
or said the same thing in two essays—for one cannot always be original
—I have eliminated one of the redundant passages. The footnotes
have been thinned and weeded; source references have been re-

tained, but most of the more discursive footnotes have been reluctantly sacrificed. At a few points where recent scholarship has produced new ideas or uncovered new evidence, I have added footnotes. References to George Fox's *Journal* and the writings of William Penn have been standardized; the reader is now referred to the best and most available recent editions. In other respects the essays remain substantially as originally written.

Contents

Contents

CHAPTER I

The Atlantic Community of the Early Friends

The Society of Friends came into existence a little more than three centuries ago, when George Fox, a religious seeker, grew dissatisfied with the dusty answers he got from the official spiritual guides of his day, and listened to an inward voice. "There is one, even Christ Jesus," the voice told him, "that can speak to thy condition."[1] It was not a new discovery in Christian history, this revelation of the inward Christ, the Light Within, but it was a momentous one for Anglo-American culture. For, as William Penn put it, what "people had been vainly seeking without with much pains and cost, they by this ministry found within . . . viz., the right way to peace with God; for they were directed to the light of Jesus Christ within them as the seed and leaven of the Kingdom of God, near all because in all, and God's talent to all: a faithful and true witness and just monitor in every bosom. . . ."[2] It was the historic role of the Quaker movement which Fox founded to revive the religion of firsthand experience, a type of religion that was in danger of being lost in the aridities of Anglican formalism and the mazes of Puritan intellectualism.

Fox was no philosopher, but he grasped instinctively the radical principle of "Occam's razor"—the principle that intellectual distinctions and subtleties are not to be multiplied indefinitely. For him it was enough that the eternal Christ, the immanent Word, was present in the soul of every man. He preached no distinctive doctrines aside from the central doctrine of the Inward Light, for theological doctrines, he believed, were merely intellectual "notions," which men were all too prone to substitute for the reality of firsthand experience. It was the practical outworkings of the Light Within—"testimonies," the Quakers called them—not a set of beliefs, that set the "Children of the Light" apart from the "world's people." Apostolic simplicity of

1

life, the practice of equality in all human relationships, love for all mankind, even one's enemies, the sharing of material and spiritual goods—these were the practical consequences of "living in the Light," and these were the distinctive marks of the Quaker way of life.

Over the years some of these religious testimonies ceased to represent fresh, original responses to the Light; inevitably they tended to become somewhat stylized, to harden into traditions, so that today some people think of the Quakers as a small, archaic sect given to the wearing of bonnets and broad-brimmed hats, the use of *thee* instead of *you*, conscientious objection to military service, and a tightly knit, exclusive group life. Yet these are simply particular manifestations—some of them, like the queer hats and the "plain language," already obsolescent—of a basic religious ethos derived from the very heart of the primitive Christian teaching. Indeed, the early Friends themselves called their movement "primitive Christianity revived," and most historians, even those most unfriendly to the Friends, have tended to agree.[3]

There are undoubtedly other movements in Christian history which can lodge an equal or a stronger claim to represent "primitive Christianity revived." Yet in spite of the frequent failure of Quakers to live up to this high calling, it is still true that there is no better opportunity to observe the primitive Christian ethos in practice under the conditions of modern life than by studying the history of the Society of Friends. Nearly a century ago, Ralph Waldo Emerson, a "friend of the Friends," remarked that "the sect of Quakers in their best representatives appear to me to come nearer to the sublime history and genius of Christ than any other of the sects. They have kept the traditions perhaps for a longer time, kept the early purity . . . and . . . I think I find in the language of that sect in all its history . . . a certain fidelity to the Christian character."[4]

One fact sets the Quakers apart from certain other groups, such as the Mennonites, which have perhaps been more consistent in their adherence to the primitive Christian ideal: even in their most secluded period—the eighteenth century—the Quakers have never withdrawn completely from the world, but have always felt it a religious duty to work out their testimonies in the midst of life. Consequently, in the essays which make up this volume our subject will be not simply Quakerism *over against* the culture of the modern world,

criticizing and at times rejecting it, but also Quakerism as *part* of that
culture, interacting with it in ways that were often creative. We shall
focus our attention particularly upon the four basic testimonies of
simplicity, equality, peace, and community, for it is at these points
that Quakerism comes most sharply into conflict with modern culture,
sometimes modifying it, sometimes being modified by it.

But first we need to define, at least in geographical terms, the culture we are talking about. The principal scene of Quaker history during its first century and a half was the enormous area bordering the
North Atlantic basin. The culture we are dealing with therefore is
the culture of the "Atlantic Community."

We first became familiar with the idea of the Atlantic Community
as a strategic concept during the Second World War, but the Atlantic
Community as a cultural fact was a matter of almost everyday experience to English-speaking people in the seventeenth and eighteenth centuries. Historians, long accustomed to arranging the data
of cultural history in patterns set by later political boundaries, have
only recently begun to realize this and to treat the Atlantic civilization
as a single unit. Nowhere is the cultural unity of the North Atlantic
littoral more apparent than in the little world of the Society of Friends.
Within the broad setting of the first British Empire the Friends
created a distinctive community—a spiritual *imperium in imperio*—
which outlasted the breakup of the old British Empire and still per-
sists to a remarkable degree in the modern world.

The principal cement of the Atlantic Quaker community was the
traveling ministry. It was one of George Fox's earliest "openings"
from the Lord that the essential qualification for a religious ministry
was not a university education but a spiritual gift and an irresistible
"concern" to preach. Such a gift might be vouchsafed to anyone—
housewife, farmer, shoemaker, merchant—regardless of his or her
mundane calling. And such a "concern" could well carry one thousands of miles to the far corners of the North Atlantic world. Fox
might have added a stout constitution and a courageous spirit to the
qualifications for the Quaker ministry, but he was sure the Lord
would fortify His prophets with the hardihood their labors required.

The Quaker ministers, constantly circulating through the vast
Atlantic world, were not only messengers of the gospel of the Inward
Light; they were cultural "carriers" who helped to hold the larger

Atlantic Community together. Today the Society of Friends, still infinitesimally small as compared with the major Protestant denominations, has become world-wide in its outreach, with active meetings on every continent, though its principal strength is still in the English-speaking world. A special Quaker organization, the Friends World Committee for Consultation, now exists for the purpose of carrying on the work of those tireless early travelers. By encouraging intercommunication among Friends across the world, it bears witness to the validity of George Fox's momentous insight of three centuries ago—that God speaks in every human heart and that this common religious experience transcends all political and cultural boundaries.

1

In the spring of 1652, George Fox climbed to the top of Pendle Hill in Lancashire and caught a prophetic vision of "a great people to be gathered," a "people in white raiment . . . coming to the Lord."[5] With this hilltop vision the history of the Society of Friends begins. For, descending from the hill, Fox found in the nearby towns of Sedbergh, Kendal, and Preston Patrick those waiting communities of Seekers which under his ministry became the nucleus of a religious society whose members called one another "Friends in the Truth." Surely those North Country Seekers were the people in white raiment of Fox's vision. And unquestionably the crowded month which Fox spent in North Lancashire, Westmorland, and the West Riding of Yorkshire was "the creative moment in the history of Quakerism."[6]

Having said this, I hope I may be indulged in a brief flight of the historical fancy. I should like to suggest another interpretation of Fox's vision from Pendle Hill. "When I came atop of it," he wrote, "I saw Lancashire sea. . . ." In other words, he faced westward—toward the open ocean and the setting sun. It is a tenuous clue, an insubstantial peg on which to hang a historical thesis, and I do not wish to be taken more than half seriously. Still, I wonder whether in his vision from the top of Pendle Hill, Fox could have foreseen another harvest of souls, farther in the future, in fields remote from northern England, but just as dramatic, just as fateful, and, in the end, vastly more extensive. Could it have been beyond the sea, beyond the Atlantic, in the half-known lands to the west and southwest, that Fox saw "a great people to be gathered"?

It is a mere speculation, a highly problematic one at best.[7] But whether or not Fox, standing on Pendle Hill that spring day, glimpsed the transatlantic world in his mind's eye, it is a fact, and a momentous one, that hardly three years were to pass before adventurous "publishers of Truth" were going over to possess that land. By the time of Fox's death, forty years later, there would be Quaker communities in every part of the British colonies in America. In numbers the transatlantic Friends would nearly equal those in Great Britain. Let another half-century pass, and the Quaker population of the New World would have outstripped that of the home island. "Westward the course of empire takes its way." Westward too the main current of Quaker expansion, a current destined to carry George Fox's message across the broad Atlantic, across a vast continent, to the rim of another sea, the far-off Pacific.

It is not with that mighty expansive surge, however, that I am primarily concerned. It is rather with the process by which Friends on both sides of the Atlantic came to feel that they were members of a single community, an Atlantic community of Friends.

2

If the man who stood on Pendle Hill in 1652 was looking westward, he was one of the few Englishmen at that moment who were doing so. Most English eyes just then were turned anxiously toward the continent or toward Whitehall and Westminster. In the Narrow Seas war was raging with the Dutch. At home trouble was brewing between the Rump Parliament and the Army. The end of the Commonwealth was in sight, with Cromwell's Protectorate over the horizon. Englishmen were giving little thought to the New World in 1652.[8]

The half-century just closed had witnessed a vigorous burst of British colonizing activity. It had seen the occupation of New England, of the Chesapeake Bay region, of the outer rim of Caribbean islands. The half-century to come would be another period of strenuous colonizing effort. It would see the conquest of Jamaica from the Spanish, of the Hudson River region from the Dutch, the peaceful settlement of the Carolinas, the Jerseys, of Pennsylvania. But meanwhile there was a pause, and Englishmen concentrated on urgent home problems.

A distinguished American historian has observed that this pause marked the beginning of a profound alteration in English intellectual and spiritual life, the final casting off of the medieval outlook and the assumption of the modern. "The heroic age of Puritanism had passed," says Charles M. Andrews. Englishmen now began to "emancipate" themselves from the religious preoccupations of the past. They began to look about them with new eyes, in a scientific and commercial spirit, *this* world, not the next, the focus of their attention.[9] When the English nation resumed its colonizing work, Andrews says, it would do so in a new and different mental climate, the secular, scientific, materialistic atmosphere of the world we know.

As such historical generalizations go, this observation is probably sound. But the Quaker historian must add a qualification with his endorsement. The heroic age of Quakerism was just beginning. The "Children of the Light," who would presently swarm from the North Country into every corner of the British Isles and out to the uttermost parts of the sea, combined something of the old outlook with something of the new. They had all the burning religious zeal, all the passion for righteousness, of the earlier Puritans, but at the same time their outlook was remarkably congenial to the commercial and scientific spirit of the new age. The Friends of the 1650's were peculiarly equipped to bridge the gap between the two periods of British colonization.

But this is to look at history with the perspective of the present. We need to know how the New World appeared to George Fox and his contemporaries in 1652.

If they had but little accurate information about the Western world, the fact is hardly surprising. Few Englishmen of their time had more than a hazy conception of the continent across the Atlantic. "The first adequate geographical treatise written in English, entirely devoted to describing the American lands,"[10] appeared in 1651, the year before George Fox climbed Pendle Hill. It is doubtful whether Fox or any of the early Friends read George Gardyner's *A Description of the New World.* Still, we may turn to it for a picture of the American world as it appeared to English eyes in the 1650's.

First landfall to the westward was the island of Newfoundland, eternally wrapped in fogs, its lofty beetling cliffs a forbidding sight to the Atlantic voyager. There was little about the island, said Gardyner, "to invite a Plantation, it is so Rockie and barren." At most a few hundred fisherfolk pieced out a scanty living there. Newfoundland stood guard over the mouth of the St. Lawrence River. Far up that majestic estuary one might come upon a few French fur traders, exchanging guns, blankets, and gewgaws with the Indians for beaver skins.

Southwestward lay New England, a collection of communities hugging a rocky shoreline and boasting after three decades of settlement perhaps fifty thousand souls.[11] Gardyner knew of only three political divisions within New England—a string of tiny fishing communities called Maine, the flourishing Puritan colony of Boston or Massachusetts Bay, and the little Separatist colony of New Plymouth, whose heroic days now lay behind it. It was typical of the prevailing ignorance about the New World that even a well-informed geographer like Gardyner knew nothing of New Hampshire's fifteen-mile strip of coast with its mountainous back country, of the Providence Plantations, where Roger Williams had created a haven of religious toleration; of the two Puritan outposts of Connecticut and New Haven. Gardyner, it is clear, was not much taken with New England: "generally barren and rocky," he had found it, a place, moreover, where the people "punish sin as severely as the *Jews* did in old time, but not with so good a warrant."

New Holland, the Dutch trading colony on the Hudson, comprised a few "plantations" and "but one Village"—the hamlet which would one day be New York. Adjacent Long Island was Dutch at one end, English at the other; both governments claimed it, "but at present," Gardyner said dryly, "the Inhabitants live without duty to either." Below the Dutch settlement stretched a broad expanse of primeval forest, untenanted save for a handful of Swedes and Finns along Delaware Bay and the remnants of a once-powerful Indian people, the Lenni Lenape. New Jersey, Pennsylvania, Delaware were still undreamed of.

Maryland was a province with a future, but very little to show in the present—a few thousand Englishmen scattered along the upper reaches of Chesapeake Bay. But its Roman Catholic Proprietor had decreed toleration there, and Gardyner's opinion was that "it is likely to be a flourishing Countrey." Virginia was a cluster of tobacco plantations along lower Chesapeake Bay and the "divers Rivers" which emptied into it. But the climate was unwholesome, the swamps infested with rattlesnakes "whose bitings are present death." Nor was there much to be said, in Gardyner's view, for the inhabitants, who numbered perhaps twenty thousand: "I think," he said, "they are the farthest from conscience and morall honesty, of any such number together in the world." Passing southward from Virginia, one came into a region which the geographer pronounced "farre beyond" any other land on the main for climate and natural resources. Unhappily, this land of Eden was inaccessible and all but uninhabited because of its rocky capes and the "shelvy ground" along the coast.

There, in the silent forests of what was to be North Carolina, the British mainland empire ended. Miles to the south, in Florida, stood a few outposts of the Spanish king. Across the Gulf of Mexico lay the "kingdoms" of New Spain, a vast realm extending all the way to the remote Straits of Magellan, a region which the average Englishman, if he was conscious of it at all, regarded as mysterious and hostile, fabulously wealthy, but sunk in popery, barbarism, and slavery.

The real heart of the British empire lay offshore. Bermuda, or the Somers Islands, despite the "blustring winds, which often haunteth their coasts," wrote Gardyner, was "a most wholsome place to live in, and wel replenished with our Nation." Tiny British islands—the Bahamas, the Leeward Islands, Barbados—defined the outer rim of the warm Caribbean. Barbados, chief of the sugar islands, was Britain's richest colony: "it flourisheth so much," said Gardyner, "that it hath more people and Commerce then all the Ilands of the *Indies*." Directly south, on the coast of South America, was Surinam, or Guiana. Its aboriginal people, our geographer proudly reported, "love our Nation above any other."[12] Even as Gardyner's book was in press, Englishmen were planting a tiny settlement there.

This was the western rim of the North Atlantic world in 1652, when George Fox stood atop Pendle Hill—a broken string of settlements stretching from Newfoundland in the north to Surinam in the south and containing perhaps two hundred thousand English-speaking inhabitants. This was the New World into which Quaker missionaries were about to venture. This was the region in which, George Fox tells us, "truth broake foorth" in 1656.[13]

3

The story of the Quaker pioneers in America has often been told. It is an epic of ordinary men and women, who had only their courage, their devotion, their calm faith to pit against all the obstacles that nature and man's inhumanity could raise against them. It is a story that deserves to be told again and again. But it is not my story. I must be content to extract from it two or three observations which have a direct bearing on my theme.

The first phase of Quaker activity in the New World lasted from 1655 to 1662. The number of Friends who crossed the Atlantic in that eight-year period is so large as to suggest that the publishing of Truth in America was a major enterprise of the infant Society of Friends. No less than sixty men and women carried the Quaker message to the New World in that brief span of years. Into every British colony they carried it, from cold, foggy Newfoundland, where Hester Biddle touched shore in 1656, to the steaming jungles of Surinam, which John Bowron penetrated a year later.[14] That such a large-scale missionary operation could have been initiated and carried on by a society so recently founded is an extraordinary testimony to the power of religious faith in the lives of the first Quakers.

It was a spontaneous effort, this movement out across the waters. No executive body planned it, no consultative committee coordinated it, for the Children of the Light had no such central organs. If there were any planning and guidance, it came from Margaret Fell's home at Swarthmoor Hall and later from the General Meetings in the northern counties, which gave spiritual support and some financial aid.[15] The concern to carry the Quaker message beyond seas was an inevitable extension of the impulse which had sent the first "publishers of Truth" out of the North Country in the spring of 1654 to scatter their seed broadcast over the nation.

The amazing thing is how quickly the overseas work began. The first Quaker ministers had been in Bristol barely a year before one of them was writing back in 1655 to Swarthmoor Hall that "Many are

raised up and moved for several parts; here are four from hereaway
moved to go for New England, two men and two women; some are
gone for France, and some for Holland."[16]

The references to France and Holland remind us that these "publishers of Truth" did not confine their overseas work to North America
alone. The Inner Light was universal, and the evangelical drive of
early Quakerism was world-wide in scope.[17] "Let all nations hear
the sound by word or writing," George Fox urged. "Be patterns, be
examples, in all countries, places, islands, nations . . . then you will
come to walk cheerfully over the world, answering that of God in
every one."[18] The same impulse which sent sixty Friends westward to
the New World sent others—a smaller number—to the eastward,
into the Low Countries and on into northern Germany, north into
Scandinavia, south into France and Italy, and on to the eastern
Mediterranean.

Every Quaker knows the romantic stories of Mary Fisher before
the sultan, of poor John Love before the pope, of George Robinson's
exciting adventures on the road to Jerusalem, of George Fox's letters
to the Emperor of Muscovy, the Great Turk, the Emperor of China,
the Grand Cham of Tartary, and Prester John, the fabulous ruler of
the East. There is great charm in these stories, and undeniable symbolic value. Yet no one would argue that their historical significance is
great.

The fact is that though the first Friends sowed their seed broadcast, they did not reap a harvest everywhere. Beyond the area peopled
by Europeans the seed fell by the wayside, and was trodden down
or devoured. In the countries of southern Europe it fell among thorns,
and was choked out by an authoritarian church and an alien habit
of religious thinking. Even in northern Europe the Quaker seed fell
in stony places; a few meetings quickly sprang up—in Amsterdam,
Rotterdam, Friedrichstadt, Danzig—but "they had not much earth,"
and sooner or later (though some of them lasted for a century or
more) they withered away.

It was chiefly in North America that the seed was to bring forth
abundant and lasting fruit. Why in North America? Because there, I
suggest, the ground was prepared in a special, an essential way.
Quakerism in England had flowered out of Puritan soil. Geoffrey
Nuttall has shown us that it was not a revolt against Puritanism, as we

used to think, not a rejection of the ultra-Protestant religious ethos, but a special development, a distinctive emphasis within the Puritan tradition, and in a real sense the fulfillment of it.[19]

Now British North America was a nursery of Puritanism, a hot-bed in which it flourished in all its profusion of varieties and sub-varieties. Everyone knows that New England was Puritan to the core. But there were little colonies of emigrant New Englanders everywhere—on Long Island, in northern New Jersey, in Maryland, Virginia, and North Carolina. And even those Americans who were not transplanted New Englanders were likely to be Puritans in the broader sense. The majority of settlers in Maryland, for instance, were not Roman Catholics like their Proprietors, but Protestants of Puritan tendencies. The Establishment in Virginia was distinctly "low church" in nature, more Protestant than Catholic, more Puritan than Anglican.[20] And even the Dutch burghers of New Amsterdam were Calvinists, close in spirit to the English Puritans.

All over North America, then, Puritanism acted as a conditioning agent, preparing the ground, providing that fertilizing, life-sustaining element that was apparently needed to make the Quaker seed germinate.[21] In this Puritan soil grew all or nearly all of the varieties of religious experience which made Commonwealth England such a fantastic and fascinating garden of spiritual blooms. There were Congregationalists and Separatists, Anabaptists and Antinomians, Seekers and Ranters. There were some sects—Gortonites, Rogerenes—which had no precise counterpart in England but represented the same reaching toward the freedom of the Spirit that marked left-wing Puritanism there.[22] Quakerism, then, was as natural, as inevitable a growth across the Atlantic as it was in England. No wonder that the sixty first "publishers of Truth" in North America found such a receptive seedbed for their message.[23]

The eight years of expansion were followed by eight years of sore persecution at home, persecution so bitter that the Society of Friends needed all its strength merely to survive. During this dark and troublous period, the stream of Quaker visitors to America dwindled to a bare trickle.[24]

By 1671, however, "persecution began to cease."[25] Rumors were afloat that dissenters might soon have freedom of worship, that proposals for a limited toleration were being discussed in high places.[26]

The storm appeared to be lifting, though the respite was only temporary. Now to George Fox came the word of the Lord that he should "goe beyonde ye seas Into America & Barbadoes & those countryes."[27] It was one of the most momentous "openings" in Fox's career. It began a new chapter in Anglo-American Quakerism.

Fox and his twelve companions—the number was surely not accidental—landed at Barbados early in October, 1671. Separating into groups, they set about to visit every part of the British Empire in America. Their primary objective was to extend over the New World the system of Monthly Meetings which Fox had been diligently settling throughout England during the preceding four years. But they were still "publishers of Truth," and their purpose was also evangelistic. With evident satisfaction Fox writes of the crowds of people, including many great figures in the "world," who flocked to hear them. In some regions, like North Carolina, where settlement was just beginning, Fox and his companions were, in the strict sense, religious pioneers, the first bearers of the Christian gospel.[28]

The temptation is strong to state categorically that Fox had a third object—to explore the vacant expanse between New York and Maryland with a view to a Quaker colonizing venture. Unfortunately, evidence for such a statement is only circumstantial. Still, the events which followed his return to England seem too closely linked to have been mere coincidence. Within a few years Friends were negotiating for the purchase of West New Jersey. Presently William Penn was drawn into the West Jersey enterprise. Friends by the hundreds set sail for the new land. Then came the purchase of East Jersey, followed closely by the grant of Pennsylvania and Delaware. Within eight years the wilderness which Fox had twice traversed, the great middle region stretching from the mouth of the Hudson to the mouth of the Delaware, was in Quaker hands. Meanwhile, Rhode Island to the northeastward and North Carolina to the south had become, to all intents and purposes, Quaker colonies.

All this is familiar enough. I mention it only to drive home a point: that from 1670 on, the eyes of English Friends were pretty steadily turned westward. The great men of the Society were concerned with overseas affairs. The Meeting for Sufferings, established at London in 1676, devoted much of its time to problems relating to the western "plantations." The flow of ministering Friends across the Atlantic revived: hardly a year went by that did not find from two to six "public Friends" on the high seas, traveling to or from America. And every year from the north of England, from London and Bristol, from the West Country, from Wales, from Ireland, and from Holland, scores and hundreds of Friends were migrating to the Delaware Valley to participate in the "holy experiment," aware, as Fox constantly reminded them, that there they would be as a city set on a hill. Letters from emigrant friends and relations, reports from returned travelers, epistles from colonial Yearly Meetings, all served to keep America in the consciousness of those who stayed behind.

This incessant traveling back and forth across the Atlantic, this Quaker folk migration, this steady concern with the "progress of Truth" beyond seas had its repercussions in English Quakerism. No such drastic redistribution of population could occur without dislocation, unsettlement, and confusion. The basic question of whether Truth was advanced by emigration gave rise to sharp controversy among Friends.[29] And indeed the immediate results of emigration were sometimes crippling or debilitating to the Society at home. What Welsh Friends called "runnings to Pennsylvania" seriously weakened the meetings in Wales, and the exodus of the younger, more vigorous Friends had a similar effect on meetings elsewhere. Indeed, in W. C. Braithwaite's opinion, this steady drain on the strength of British meetings was one cause of the lapse into Quietism that presently took place.[30]

But if Friends found themselves spread more thinly over a wider area, they compensated for the loss of compact strength by forging bonds which held them tightly together over that vast area. If George Fox's greatest achievement was "the knitting together of Friends into a great religious society,"[31] then the consummation of that achievement was the successful extension of the society across the Atlantic, making Friends wherever they found themselves—in Antigua, Jamaica, New Jersey, Maryland, Rhode Island, in London, Bristol, Yorkshire, Ireland, Holland—feel that they were all members of the same society.

4

It remained for our time to coin the phrase "Atlantic Community" —and we have given it overtones that are alien to the spirit of

Quakerism and its peace testimony. But the early Friends knew the reality of an Atlantic community, a community held together by the intangible yet powerful bonds of love, fellowship, and a common faith.

More than anything else it was the traveling ministry that welded Friends around the Atlantic rim into one people.[32] I have already spoken of the ministers' activity in "publishing the Truth" throughout the colonial world. That was a missionary service. But they had also a pastoral function—to tend the widely scattered flock, to nourish the meetings, keep them alive and healthy, to infuse new strength when needed.

Nearly a hundred and fifty men and women—almost as many women as men—braved the Atlantic in the half-century after 1652 to spend a year, two years, sometimes three or four years visiting the American meetings. Many of these Atlantic travelers left personal records of their peregrinations. Among them none is more affecting, none more revealing than that of Joan Vokins. Her brief journal lacks the sustained exaltation and historical importance of Fox's, the blunt power of William Edmundson's, the narrative skill of Thomas Ellwood's, the learning and rich detail of Thomas Story's. But it has its own naïve and poignant charm, and if we want to know how the Atlantic Quaker community was sustained and strengthened year by year, we shall learn more perhaps from the experiences of a simple "handmaid of the Lord" like Joan Vokins than from those of the more famous Friends.

The mother of seven children, frail and sickly in body, well advanced in years, this Berkshire Friend, from West Challow, felt an unmistakable call toward the end of the 1670's to cross the sea "in the love of the Gospel." She struggled against the unwelcome summons, but she found "the Hand of the All-wise God" so heavy upon her that she "could no longer stay at home, although both sick and lame, and much to undergo both inwardly and outwardly." It was wintertime and she was but a fragile old woman, yet she "did not dare to plead with the Lord any longer, or to make any Excuse." So she took ship and set off across the wild Atlantic.

It was May, 1680, when she landed at New York, exhausted by the long voyage. She found Friends on Long Island in a turmoil. Ranters, she discovered, "were very abusive in those remote Islands," disturbing meetings with their "antick tricks." Weak as she was, and "near unto death," she mustered enough strength to go to the General Meeting, leaning on the arms of two women Friends. Once in the meetinghouse, she felt herself so filled with the Lord's power that she was able to stand up and put the mischievous Ranters to silence and to shame.

From Long Island she traveled to Providence for four crowded days of Rhode Island General Meeting and thence by sea to Boston, where the meetings were unexpectedly peaceable. One of her hearers there was "a *Lawyer* that had a hand in the suffering of our *Friends* that were put to Death." But those grim days were twenty years behind, and the persecutor had apparently repented, for she found him "very solid."

Back now through Rhode Island to Long Island. There she took shipping for East Jersey, on whose treacherous shoals her vessel was almost wrecked. She passed from meeting to meeting in East and West Jersey, then crossed the Delaware to Pennsylvania—"but it had not that Name then"—and helped organize the meetings which William Penn was to find already functioning when he landed in his province.

Now at last she was "clear," her religious duty discharged—or so she thought. She started back to New York to take passage for England, pleased at the prospect of seeing her children and her Berkshire home again. But suddenly the Lord revealed that He had further work for her. He laid it upon her to go to Barbados, which, she confesses, "was no little Cross to my Mind." But it was the Lord's will and she was His faithful handmaid. So off to Barbados she sailed.

While she was on the high seas, her sailing directions were changed: she must visit Friends in the Leeward Islands. Again it was the Lord's will—"so he carried the Vessel, let them that sail'd do what they could: and they could not steer their Course *Barbadoes-Road,* altho they endeavoured it with all their might." The ship lay to at Antigua for a week before the annoyed owner, "a hypocritical Professor," would let her go ashore. When at length he relented, she had "a precious time" with the "little handful of plain-hearted Friends" on the island.

Now that her service was completed at Antigua, the master could turn his vessel's prow again towards Barbados. But, lo, it came into

Joan's heart to visit Friends at Nevis, and willy-nilly the owner saw his bark carried thither. By now he was thoroughly exasperated. He refused to drop anchor, but insisted on heading once more for Barbados. For three weeks he sought to weather the point of the island, but he could make no headway against the winds, "for the Hand of the Lord was against him."

Frustrated, baffled, enraged, the captain put Joan ashore on the rocky isle of Montserrat. The little Quaker community on the island had been uprooted and scattered; the people now, she discovered, "were generally *Irish* Papists." No matter: the indomitable Quakeress "published Truth in the Streets" of Montserrat, and then took passage on a "leaking Vessell" for Antigua. From Antigua she finally made her way to Nevis and "had many good and powerful Meetings."

The end of her long, arduous journey was in sight. It was early in 1681 when she finally reached Barbados. She visited all the meetings on that island, finding special service among the Negro slaves. Now at last she was "clear." Now she could return to her Berkshire home, to her children, her own meeting. When she landed in England after all these extraordinary adventures, the frail old Quakeress had been gone nearly a year and a half.[33]

The heroism, the fortitude, the persistence, the unfailing devotion of "public Friends" like Joan Vokins held the Atlantic Quaker community together. To remote clearings in Carolina pine forests, to tiny Caribbean islands swept by trade winds, to raw, new settlements on the banks of the Delaware they came, bringing a fresh ministry, bringing word of the "progress of Truth" in other parts, bringing news from "home," welcome news of friends and kinsfolk, giving Quakers in every corner of the Atlantic world a sense of belonging to a single body, of being members one of another.

Other influences carried on and supplemented the work of the traveling ministers. As the epistles of Paul and James, Peter and John had shaped and nourished the early Christian community of the Mediterranean, so the epistles of George Fox, Margaret Fell, Josiah Coale, John Burnyeat, William Edmundson gave spiritual sustenance and practical advice to the far-flung Quaker community of the Atlantic. As soon as there were Yearly Meetings in existence on both sides of the ocean, there began that regular interchange of epistles that has continued down to the present. It was a day when the average person, especially in the colonies, saw the written or printed word but seldom. The impact of these epistles was therefore vastly greater than it could possibly be in our day, when printed matter threatens to overwhelm us.

In 1684 Philadelphia Yearly Meeting wrote to London: "We dearly love and embrace you though at this outward distance. Yea, oftentimes we confer with you and meet with you in our spirits and have heavenly union with you in Christ Jesus to our great comfort, joy, and refreshment."[34] Consider the circumstances—Pennsylvania colony barely settled, hundreds of Friends nostalgically thinking of home, a new Yearly Meeting facing the difficult problems of rightly ordering its religious and social life in the wilderness. Of one thing we can be sure: authors of epistles did not have to search for "something to say," and the language they used was neither perfunctory nor forced. One still catches in these ancient epistles a sense of that emotional identification with the larger Society of Friends which was the cement of the Quaker Atlantic community.

A seventeenth century Friend in Maryland, Rhode Island, or Barbados saw few books. But the books which he did read were the same ones that his brethren in England were reading. As early as 1658 Friends in the north of England were sending books to Virginia. After George Fox's return from America, he set up regular channels for supplying American Friends with reading matter.[35] The books that went across the Atlantic—the writings of Fox himself, of Burrough, Penington, Howgill, and the other doughty penmen of early Quakerism—tended to foster a common intellectual life, a common universe of discourse, among Friends wherever they were.

Always too there was that sense of intimate and purposeful fellowship that comes from mutual aid, from sharing one's material goods with those in need. At first, quite naturally, financial contributions flowed westward. In 1656 Margaret Fell was stirring up North Country Friends to contribute to the Kendal fund "for the service of Truth." It was the "stock" raised in this region that helped send the first "publishers of Truth" across the sea.[36] In 1672, when interest in transatlantic Quakerism was reviving, during a lull in the storm of persecution, the General Meeting held in London called upon all Friends to contribute toward "the management of Truth's affairs; particularly for Friends' supply who are called into the service of the

Lord beyond sea."³⁷ Later in the century, when Quakerism was firmly established on New World soil, American Friends were called upon to share in the common burdens—the ransoming of Quakers held captive by Barbary pirates, the relief of suffering in war-torn Ireland.³⁸

In 1691 George Fox lay on his deathbed. Nearly forty years had passed since his vision on Pendle Hill. The Atlantic community of Friends which he, more than anyone else, had shaped and nurtured, was much on his mind. Even in his last hours, William Penn tells us, he was "Recommending . . . the *Dispatch* and *Dispersion* of an *Epistle* just before Written to the *Churches of Christ*, throughout the World . . . but above all, *Friends*, and of all *Friends*, those in *Ireland* and *America*, twice over saying 'Mind poor *Friends* in *Ireland* and *America*.' "³⁹

5

More than two and a half centuries have passed since George Fox died with a concern for the transatlantic Quaker community on his heart. That community has survived in spite of many vicissitudes— theological tensions and divisions within, political tensions and divisions without.⁴⁰

The eighteenth century saw the maturing of American Quakerism, saw its achievement of something like equal partnership in the Atlantic Quaker community. The center of population shifted decisively to the west, though the center of gravity—in the Quaker sense of "weight"—remained in England. What a Rhode Island Friend told an English minister early in the century could have been said as well at the end—even after the Declaration of Independence: "They in that Country looked upon themselves but as the Daughters, and Friends here in Old England as their Mother."⁴¹ Philadelphia Yearly Meeting, for example, regularly consulted London on such important matters as participation in the slave trade or in provincial politics. The traveling ministry—most potent influence for cohesion—became a reciprocal force. Americans like John Churchman, Samuel Emlen, and Job Scott came to be as well known in English meetings as Samuel Bownas, Catherine Payton Phillips, and Samuel Fothergill were among American Friends. As Quaker merchants established themselves in Philadelphia, New York, and Newport, they entered into business relations with their opposite numbers in London, Bristol, Plymouth, and Cork, and the powerful cement of trade was added to the other, less tangible forces that held the Quaker community together.

Of the nineteenth century it is more difficult to speak, for it has been neglected by Quaker historians. Superficially, the North Atlantic Quaker community was still one. Ministers crossed the ocean in both directions. Yearly Meetings exchanged epistles regularly. Humanitarian causes—the relief of famine in Ireland, the abolition of Negro slavery—enlisted the efforts of concerned Friends everywhere. But there were obvious fissures in the unity of the Society of Friends. American Quakerism was fragmented, shattered. There was no longer *one* Society, and this sad fact set sharp limits to the effectiveness of the old cohesive forces.[42]

Transatlantic Quakerism had survived the political convulsions of the American Revolution almost unimpaired. But it could not avoid the impact of the nineteenth century's pervasive nationalism. Moreover, American Quakers, like most of their countrymen, were looking westward, not eastward. They were *moving* westward, as they had been doing steadily since the seventeenth century, absorbed in the great enterprise of peopling a continent. It was, perhaps, natural that the old Atlantic community, the traditional ties with London Yearly Meeting, should fade from consciousness, displaced for the moment by more urgent interests. How it was with British Friends, how real the old Atlantic community seemed in the age of the new industrialism at home and the new empire in the East, I shall not venture to say. But certainly Friends in the British Isles were looking eastward, as the process of English colonization carried Quakerism to Australasia and South Africa, as new Quaker communities came into being in Scandinavia, France, Switzerland, Germany, and Holland. Indeed, all this was in some degree a revival of the eastward expansive impulse of the earliest Friends.

The first half of the twentieth century has seen, I think, something of a revival, a renewal of the Atlantic community in the Society of Friends. I shall merely mention the steady cooperation among British, American, and Continental Friends in relief work, of the recent activity of international Quaker "teams" at the United Nations, of the three great conferences—London in 1920, Swarthmore in 1937, Ox-

ford in 1952—which have brought Friends from all over the world
face to face.

Prophecy is hazardous. The wise historian avoids it and confines
himself to the past, his proper domain. But I shall rashly venture the
forecast that international Quaker cooperation will increase in the
coming years, that this mutual interaction will strengthen Quakerism
on both sides of the Atlantic, and will enable the Society of Friends
to become a more effective force in the world. There is a new role,
an important role waiting to be filled by a revived Atlantic community of Friends.

In the world at large the Atlantic Community is becoming a reality
again in our time. Partly this is a natural growth, the product of in-
eluctable forces which have reduced the size of our planet and made
us all neighbors. But partly it is a forced growth. It stems from political circumstances which have divided our world in two. It is cultivated for political and strategic purposes with which Friends can
have little sympathy. Within the somewhat arbitrary and externally
imposed framework of this new Atlantic community, a voluntary,
organic, functional Quaker community can keep alive a different
ideal, can demonstrate another pattern of international cooperation,
one that is motivated by love, not fear, one that is not exclusive, not
directed *against* anyone or anything, any nation or any group of
nations.

In the effort to recover and renew the Atlantic community of
Friends, the historians can be of service. They can restudy the Quaker
past in a new light. Forgetting arbitrary boundaries, boundaries that
did not exist during the first century and a quarter of Quakerism, and
had no real meaning to Friends for years after that, the historians can
give us a view of the Society of Friends as it actually appeared to
George Fox and his successors—a single religious community co-
extensive in a geographical sense with the greater Atlantic world of
the British Empire, but annexed in a spiritual sense to the Kingdom
of Heaven.

CHAPTER II

The Transatlantic Quaker Community in the Seventeenth Century: Its Structure and Functioning

Early Quakerism is commonly regarded as a manifestation of extreme individualism in religion. It is easy enough to understand how this interpretation should have arisen. In their search for a source of authority, George Fox and his successors turned away from the outward letter of the Scriptures, the typical Protestant's warrant for religious truth, and away from an outward church, to which the Catholic looked for the same assurance. They found what they were seeking in the Divine Light shining in their own souls. Every man, they insisted, had immediate access to a private source of Truth, or, as Thomas Hobbes, an unfriendly critic, put it, "Every boy or wench thought he spoke with God Almighty."[1] What is this, one naturally asks, but sheer anarchic individualism, unrestrained, unmitigated, unabashed? This is precisely what the orthodox Puritan or Anglican asked in the seventeenth century, and the answer he invariably gave was summed up in the title of an anti-Quaker tract of 1660: *Hell Broke Loose; or, An History of the Quakers.*

But actually, nothing is more striking in the faith and practice of the early Friends than their strong and abiding sense of *community.* The Inward Light to which the Quaker appealed was not a different light for each individual, but the one true Light "that lighteth every man that cometh into the world." The sense of participation in a common religious experience with other "Children of the Light" created a solidarity which enabled the Quaker movement to survive when most of the cognate sects of the Commonwealth period in England disintegrated and disappeared. A. Neave Brayshaw, an English

21

Quaker writer, has called attention to the frequent occurrence in early
Quaker literature of the phrase "one another" in expressions like
"mind that which is pure in one another, which joins you together,"
or "that all may be as one family, building up one another and helping
one another."[2] This "one-anotherness" was early embodied in a dis-
tinct and coherent group life; presently it was crystallized in a system
of Monthly and Quarterly Meetings "for discipline" (note the word,
which scarcely connotes unrestrained individualism). In these meetings all decisions were taken by the unanimous "sense of the meeting."

The Quaker meeting for worship, held "on the basis of silence,"
was not simply an occasion for the trimming of individual lamps; it
was an opportunity for the merging of one's light in that of a worshiping group. Robert Barclay, the Quaker theologian, expressed it in a
striking figure of speech: "As many candles lighted and put in one
place do greatly augment the light, and make it more to shine forth,
so when many are gathered together into the same life, there is more
of the glory of God and His power appears, to the refreshment of each
individual; for that he partakes not only of the light and life raised
in himself, but in all the rest."[3] In this "holy dependence of the mind
upon God," the Friends found both the highest experience of individual selfhood and the fullest experience of solidarity and shared life.

Thus his strong group-consciousness did not make the early Friend
the prototype of the "organization man" any more than it made him
a rugged spiritual individualist. What William H. Whyte calls the
"social ethic" was held in a creative tension with the "Protestant ethic"
of individualism. Here, in short, was a paradox that resolved the eternal problem of the one and the many, the individual and the group:
in losing themselves in the pregnant silence of the worshiping community they found themselves most completely.

The sense of community could also be combined in a remarkable
way with the early Quaker vision of world conquest for the Truth, as
when George Fox wrote to Friends in Barbados, Virginia, New England, and "all the islands about": "be faithful . . . be obedient to the
Truth, and spread it abroad, which must go over all the world, to
professors, Jews, Christians, and heathen, to the answering the witness of God in them all. . . . And, Friends, in the wisdom of God
dwell, which preserveth in unity in the spirit and power."[4] In the end
the hopeful world vision faded, and the Friends gave themselves in-

creasingly to the cultivation of their own spiritual garden. But that garden, as we have seen, was of vast extent, and within it they achieved a genuine community by means which the following chapter analyzes in detail.

1

The successful effort to spread Quakerism "beyond the seas" can be likened to a large-scale military operation. The comparison may seem somewhat incongruous at first sight, but the warrant for it is found in the Quaker writings themselves, where the first missionaries are described as "spiritually weaponed and armed men" going forth "to fight and conquer all nations, and bring them to the nation of God."[5] Although the Quakers declined the use of carnal weapons, they had in their spiritual armory some potent instruments of offense, not the least of which was their willingness to suffer for the glory and spread of Truth. Their Supreme Commander was on high with a direct line of communication to each of His soldiers, but a secondary headquarters was maintained at Swarthmoor Hall in a remote corner of Lancashire, where George Fox and Margaret Fell, later his wife, received a constant stream of reports from the front. Here in 1655 came the dispatch from Bristol: "Many are raised up and moved for several parts; there are four from hereaway moved to go for New England, two men and two women."[6] The invasion was on.

If one had an animated map of the Atlantic world, it would show Quaker beachheads being established in rapid succession in every one of the British provinces between 1655 and 1660. In some sectors, notably the peripheral colonies of Surinam and Newfoundland, the attack was apparently repulsed, or perhaps the objective did not seem worth the expenditure of strength.[7] In the other areas from Barbados on the south to the Piscataqua region on the north, the invaders fanned out from their landing places and in an astonishingly short time established viable Quaker communities in Barbados, the Leeward Islands, Jamaica, the Bahamas, Bermuda, Virginia, Maryland,

New York, Rhode Island, Massachusetts Bay, New Hampshire, and
Maine. The longest and hardest battle was fought in Massachusetts,
where by 1660 four Quakers had actually been put to death, but as
early as 1658 a Friend writing "from a Lion's Den called Boston
Prison" was able to report, using the military metaphor: "We have
2 strong places in this land, ye one at Newport in Road Iland &
ye other at Sandwitch wch ye ennemie will never get dominion
over. . . ."[8]

A second wave of invasion was launched in 1671, when George
Fox himself led a task force of twelve Quakers to the West Indies.
There they scattered, Fox sailing first to Jamaica and then to Maryland, whence he struck northward across what were to be Delaware
and New Jersey to Long Island and Providence Plantation; turning
southward again, he traveled across New Jersey and part of what was
to be Pennsylvania to Maryland and then made his way by sea and
land to Virginia and parts of the thinly settled Albemarle district of
Carolina, covering in all some sixteen thousand miles. In the wake
of this momentous journey there occurred what, at the risk of running my metaphor into the ground, I may call the first Quaker land-
ings in force—in West New Jersey after 1675 and in Pennsylvania
after 1682.

In 1655 the Society of Friends had been an insignificant sect lurk-
ing, its enemies said, in the northern fells of England "like butter-
flies."[9] By the opening of the eighteenth century it had become a
numerous and widely distributed religious body whose bounds were
virtually identical with those of the old British Empire itself. Although no estimate of population for the seventeenth century is better than a guess, it is likely that there were close to 50,000 Quakers in
the British Isles in 1700 and at least 40,000 in the Western Hemi-
sphere.[10]

2

These were the human materials. To what extent and by what
means were they shaped into a genuine community?

The most striking and effective instrumentality which the Society of Friends invented and perfected to this end was its itinerant
ministry. It is necessary to grasp the theory of the Quaker ministry
before one can understand and appreciate the manner in which it

functioned. The early Friends bore a vigorous testimony against a learned "hireling" ministry such as the Anglicans, Presbyterians, and Independents maintained. According to the Quaker theory, anyone, man or woman, adult or child, learned or illiterate, might be divinely commissioned to prophesy, that is, to preach the word of the Lord; no university training was necessary, no outward ordination was effective, and above all, no one should make a "trade" of preaching. But in practice there were certain individuals to whom were vouchsafed special gifts of prophecy; these gifts were to be cherished and cultivated; and everything possible must be done to "liberate" such ministers to travel in the service of the Gospel by providing for their expenses and those of their families while they were away from their homes and regular callings.[11]

The first Quaker apostles to reach the American colonies in the 1650's had been ministers of this sort. Once the boundaries of the Quaker community were drawn, there continued to be scores of men and women who felt a "concern" to travel in both missionary and pastoral capacities, preaching in the already established Quaker meetings and holding "appointed" meetings among the "world's people." Thus there was a constant circulation of "public Friends," as they were called, throughout the length and breadth of Quakerdom, serving almost the same function as the circulation of the blood in the animal organism, giving Friends at the remotest extremities of the Atlantic world a sense of belonging to a single body.

The enemies of the Quakers were among the first to grant the effectiveness of this itinerant ministry. Read, for instance, the plaint of a harassed missionary of the Anglican Society for the Propagation of the Gospel just after the close of the century (and make allowances, if you will, for the understandable bitterness of a newcomer to the field who finds his territory already effectively "covered" by a competing organization):

The Quakers compass sea and land to make proselytes; they send out yearly a parcel of vagabond Fellows that ought to be taken up and put in Bedlam. . . . Their preaching is of cursing and Lyes, poysoning the souls of the people with damnable errors and heresies, and not content with this in their own Territories of Pensylvania, but they travel with mischief over all parts as far as they can goe, over Virginia and Maryland, and again through Jersey and New York as far as New England. . . .[12]

The typical manner in which a concern to travel in the ministry arose may be illustrated by the example of Elizabeth Webb of Gloucestershire, England, who traveled through virtually all the American colonies toward the end of the century:

In the year 1697 [she wrote], in the sixth month, as I was sitting in the meeting in Gloucester, which was then the place of my abode, my mind was gathered into perfect stillness for some time, and my spirit was as if it had been carried away into America; and after it returned, my heart was as if it had been dissolved with the love of God, which flowed over the great ocean, and I was constrained to kneel down and pray for the seed of God in America. The concern never went out of my mind day nor night, until I went to travel there in the love of God, which is so universal that it reaches over sea and land.[13]

Once the concern had arisen, nothing was allowed to hinder its execution. After arranging his or her worldly affairs and committing his or her family to the care of God and the home meeting, the minister took shipping, usually with a companion, for some port in the colonies. In 1696 James Dickinson crossed to Virginia with the tobacco fleet and improved every opportunity to exercise his gifts en route. There were, he wrote, "above an hundred Sail in Company, the Masters of near twenty of them professed the Truth [that is, were Quakers] . . . we had several Meetings on board, and when the Weather was fair and calm, we went on board other Vessels, had Meetings, and warned the People *to repent*, directing them to *the Light of Christ, which made manifest their Sins. . . .*"[14]

Arriving in America, the minister set out on a long journey by land and water, on foot and horseback, that would carry him[15] thousands of miles, often over the roughest of trails or through trackless forests. Normally he required at least a year of traveling before he felt "clear" to return home; frequently the visits lasted two, three, or even more years. Shortly after the close of the century, one Friend calculated he had traveled 21,000 miles and visited 480 meetings in a little less than three years.[16]

There is little evidence that the itineraries were planned in advance: the ministers ordinarily trusted to divine "leadings" and "drawings" to determine which localities they should visit.[17] A few representative itineraries will provide a notion of the range of the ministers' travels. I pass over the extraordinary voyagings of Mary Fisher, who was in Barbados in 1655, in Massachusetts Bay in the next year, back in England in 1657, on the island of Nevis in 1658, and at Constantinople in 1660, ending her days in Charleston, South Carolina. A more nearly typical example from the earliest period would be Christopher Holder. This Gloucestershire Friend traveled through New England in 1656 and again in 1657; after his second visit to that inhospitable region, he sailed for the West Indies, only to return in 1658 by way of Bermuda to Rhode Island and Massachusetts Bay. After a period of imprisonment in Boston jail, he carried the Quaker message to Virginia, returning in 1659 to Rhode Island and Massachusetts, before he went back to England in 1660. Thereafter he is said to have been in America "repeatedly"; there are references in Quaker documents to at least two later visits.[18]

The travels of Roger Longworth, a Lancashireman, took him through most of the greater Atlantic world; he is described as having journeyed "six times . . . through Holland . . . also part of Germany and thereabout, several times as far as Dantzick. . . . Five times he passed through Ireland, visiting Friends. . . . Once he passed through part of Scotland, twice at Barbados, once through New England and Virginia, twice in Maryland and the Jerseys, and twice at Pennsylvania; having traveled by land above 20,000 miles and by water not much less."[19] And all this between 1675 and 1687.

The doughty William Edmundson, called by some "the great hammer of Ireland" and by others a "Boanerges or son of thunder," traveled three times through the American colonies. His route in 1671 lay through Barbados, Antigua, Barbuda, Nevis, back to Antigua and Barbados, thence to Jamaica and to Maryland, Virginia, Carolina, back through Virginia and Maryland to New York, Rhode Island, and Massachusetts, where he sailed for Ireland. On his second visit, three years later, he landed again at Barbados, where he labored for five months, and then sailed north for Rhode Island and a tour of the continental colonies which was to take him into every one of the British provinces from "Piscattaway" on the northeast to Carolina at the south. His third trip in 1683 was confined to the West Indies, where he visited Barbados, Antigua, Nevis, Montserrat, Jamaica, and Bermuda.[20]

The influence of these visitors in uniting and solidifying the Quaker community, though impossible to measure, cannot but have been powerful. "They did not merely pay a flying visit to some annual conference," writes Professor Henry J. Cadbury. "They stayed weeks in each place visiting as it came along each of the Quarterly and Monthly Meetings and often spending months in household visits to the majority of the Quaker families before they returned home or went on into the next field of labor."[21] We cannot in the very nature of the case know what news and greetings they carried from family to family, from community to community, from colony to colony, and from the mother country to the provinces and back; their journals and letters ordinarily tell only of the religious messages they bore and the spiritual state of the meetings they visited.[22] We can be sure, however, that besides the meetings for worship and the religious "opportunities" in Quaker households, there were less solemn times when the visiting Friend retailed all the news and perhaps some of the gossip he had picked up along his route or brought from England. Upon their return to England the traveling ministers normally made oral reports to the Yearly Meetings upon the state of Quakerism in the colonies, thus keeping America before the minds of those who stayed at home.

The number of Friends who crossed the Atlantic in the work of the ministry is as astonishing as the extent of their travels. I have compiled a list of 148 British Friends who traveled in America between 1655 and 1700, and there is no reason to think that my list is definitive or exhaustive. The number of travelers was largest during the great missionary effort of the late 1650's; no fewer than forty-three came to the colonies before the end of 1660. There was a falling off in the late 1660's, related, no doubt, to the severity of persecution in England under the Clarendon Code. The number of visitors rose again in the early 1670's with the great journey of George Fox and his companions, and thereafter settled down to a fairly steady rate of from two to five transatlantic visitors every year to the end of the century. Bearing in mind that each visit normally lasted more than a year, one can say that there was scarcely a time during the second half of the seventeenth century when one or more Friends from the British Isles were not traveling in some part of the American colonial world.

It was a sign of the coming of age of American Quakerism when in the 1690's a current began flowing in the opposite direction. That decade saw at least ten American Friends traveling to England under a religious concern. This reverse current was to become a steady stream in the next century, when notable Friends like John Woolman and John Pemberton were to be familiar and respected figures in English meetings.

3

If the circulating ministry can be called the bloodstream of the transatlantic Society of Friends, perhaps its bony structure can, without forcing the metaphor, be identified with the system of Monthly, Quarterly, and Yearly Meetings, to whose creation and articulation George Fox devoted so much attention.

Even in its embryonic stages, the central organization in England was concerned with Quakerism overseas. Reminiscing toward the end of his life about the first General Meetings held in the 1650's in the north of England, Fox recalled that "there we had intelligence from all parts beyond the seas, how Truth prospered and spread, both in England, Wales, Ireland, Scotland, America, Holland, and Germany."[23] The greater part of this intelligence related to the sufferings of Friends under persecution, and Fox remembered that the meetings took action to relieve them by interceding with Parliament and the king, applying to ambassadors and "great persons" in the case of persecutions outside the realm, or writing to governors in the colonies. Later this function was assigned to the specially created Meeting for Sufferings which presently became a sort of standing executive committee for the whole Society. On this committee were representatives of all the English counties; in addition, a number of Londoners, with contacts or actual experience in the colonies, were named to correspond with Friends in the West Indies and North America.[24]

In the latter part of the 1660's, Fox established all over England a system of Monthly Meetings for discipline and business, which provided the real foundation for the structure of Quaker church government whose apex was the Yearly Meeting at London. In 1668 he wrote to Friends in America, encouraging them to do likewise, and three years later made his memorable journey through the colonies with the primary object of "[bringing] the transatlantic Quaker communities into line with the Society at home, both in practice and

Church government."[25] A general Meeting was already in being in Rhode Island; and by the end of the century a network of Monthly Meetings overspread the North American colonies, culminating in Yearly Meetings held in New England, New York, Philadelphia (for Pennsylvania and New Jersey), Maryland, Virginia, and North Carolina.

The creation and elaboration of this organizational structure provided regular channels for the flow of information and ideas between mother country and colonies. A few examples from the records of the Meeting for Sufferings in London will give us a glimpse of the machinery in action. Soon after that meeting was set up in 1676 there came reports that Friends in Bermuda were in difficulties over their conscientious refusal to pay tithes to the Church of England. The Meeting for Sufferings promptly went into action: it directed the Clerk to secure copies of the latest letters patent to the Bermuda Company for study; it deputed two members to wait upon the Company authorities in London; and finally it wrote back to the Bermuda Friends that intercession was being made on their behalf. At about the same time, word came from the Barbados Quakers of a recent law preventing Negroes from attending religious meetings, and a plea was promptly made to the Lords of Trade that the law should be set aside. Next year a deputation went before the agents of the New England colonies to seek relief from persecution for Friends there, and another group waited upon the newly appointed Governor of Jamaica on a similar errand.[26] Thus through official channels the concerns, preoccupations, and needs of American Quakers were registered in the consciousness of their brethren in England.

Mutual aid, one of the prime motives behind Quaker organization, did not flow in one direction only. The plight of Quakers held captive by Barbary pirates engaged the sympathies of American Friends. The Meeting for Sufferings had only to mention the needs of these unfortunate prisoners, and American meetings responded with contributions toward their ransom. In 1689, during the troubles in Ireland following the accession of William, the Barbados Friends, who were relatively wealthy, sent £100 to be spent for the relief of suffering Quakers. By the end of the century enough wealth had accumulated in the hands of Edward Shippen, a Quaker merchant of Philadelphia, so that he was actually sending £50 in gold to

England for the benefit of "poor Friends" there—another sign of the maturing of American Quakerism.[27] The extension of the Quaker humanitarian impulse into the wider Atlantic Community beyond the Society of Friends was to come after 1700; until then Friends were necessarily preoccupied with the sufferings in their own midst.

4

The transoceanic Quaker organization existed not merely for mutual aid in the material sense, however, but also for mutual exhortation, edification, and comfort; and the spiritual community of Friends was no less real for subsisting on the plane of ideas and sentiments. What chiefly sustained this community of thought and feeling, apart from the work of the traveling ministers, was a systematic and constant transatlantic interchange of correspondence, modeled quite consciously upon the epistles which had helped shape and nourish the Christian community of the Mediterranean world in the first century.[28]

George Fox himself, nothing loath to assume the role of St. Paul, inaugurated the practice. In 1659 he composed an "Epistle General . . . to be sent abroad among the saints scattered in Old and New England, Germany, Holland, Ireland, Scotland, Barbadoes, and Virginia."[29] His general epistles were read in Monthly and Yearly Meetings all over the Atlantic world, and even those directed to specific meetings were widely circulated among other meetings, in whose record books copies may still be found.

Upon his return from his American journey in 1673, Fox suggested that Friends in Bristol undertake a regular correspondence with the American meetings, since there were frequent sailings for the colonies from that port. Still later he sought to transfer the responsibility to the newly established Yearly Meeting held at London. But although a regular correspondence was set on foot by the Yearly Meeting in 1675, American Friends continued to seek Fox's advice and he to offer it until the end of his life, and after his death in 1691 the correspondence was kept up by his widow.[30] During his lifetime Fox wrote no less than eighty-eight epistles to organized groups of Friends in America,[31] not to mention the more general ones directed "to Friends everywhere," or those addressed to individuals but clearly

intended to be shared with the recipient's meeting. Hardly a year
went by, then, but Friends in the remote plantations received a communication direct from the founder and leading figure of the Quaker
movement.

Read today, George Fox's epistles hardly seem like vibrant personal messages; indeed, they strike the modern reader as intolerably
vague and repetitious. The burden of the more general letters is:
"Mind the Light. Be faithful, be valiant for the Truth, and spread it
abroad. Keep your meetings in the power of Truth, and live together
in unity." But even these redundant exhortations doubtless came with
a special force and unction to the distant meetings of Friends in
America, for they were tangible evidence of the founder's continued
affection for them and concern for their welfare. And many of the
epistles contained specific and welcome advice on problems of
church government or difficult cases of conscience. For example, in
1657 Fox addressed an epistle to "Friends beyond sea, that have
Blacks and Indian Slaves," urging them to treat their bondservants as
children of God—incidentally one of the very earliest pleas for the
slave by a Quaker or anyone else. To Friends holding public office
in Charleston, South Carolina, he sent a cautionary reminder against
swearing oaths; to the Jamaican Friends he suggested taking advantage of a change in administration to regain the lost privilege of
affirmation; to the island of Nevis he wrote a long and important
epistle of advice to Friends who had a scruple about serving with the
local watch; to Maryland he wrote concerning the measures to be
taken with a female member who was causing trouble to the meeting.[32] Thus Fox's powerful personality exerted itself even through
the verbosity of his epistles to impress a measure of uniformity in
faith and practice upon the far-flung Quaker community.[33]

With the establishment of Yearly Meetings on both sides of the
Atlantic, new channels of correspondence were opened up. At London, wrote the creator of the system, "Friends have an account once
a year from all the Yearly Meetings in the world . . . and Friends at
the Yearly Meeting write to them at their Yearly Meetings: so that
once a year . . . God's people know the affairs of Truth . . . having
a heavenly correspondence one with another in the heavenly society
and fellowship."[34] One of the principal actions of the Yearly Meeting
for Pennsylvania and New Jersey in 1683 was to appoint a committee

to "take Care to write to the Yearly Meeting of Friends in England in order to give an Account of the Affairs of Truth here."[35] So epistles were exchanged between Yearly Meetings in the colonies as well as with London. The cumulative effect of this constant correspondence was not only to induce in individual Friends and meetings a feeling of emotional identification with the larger Quaker community but also in large measure to stereotype the thought and practice (and even the language) of that community.

This uniformity of thought was reinforced by the tendency of Friends everywhere to read the same books. The Quaker press in England was constantly busy turning out doctrinal and controversial literature which quickly found its way across the Atlantic.[36] After Fox's visit to the colonies, regular channels were set up for supplying the American Quakers with books; in 1689, for example, Philadelphia Yearly Meeting arranged with William Bradford, the printer and bookseller, to "take off" six copies of each new book published by the English Friends.[37] Bradford himself, before he fell out with his Quaker employers, reprinted a number of English Quaker publications.[38] By the end of the century the writings of American Quakers were being reprinted and presumably read in England—a further sign that Americans were moving toward something like equal partnership in the transatlantic Quaker community.[39]

5

The unity of the seventeenth century Society of Friends was temporarily shattered by three serious schisms. But even these incidents bore witness to the organic character of the transatlantic Quaker community.

Perhaps it is the leaven of individualism in the Society of Friends which has caused its history to be periodically marked by "separations." But what is more significant is the speed and completeness with which, in the seventeenth century at least, schisms were healed and the community restored to wholeness. And, paradoxically, the very course of the major "separations" supplies the best evidence of the reality of the Atlantic Quaker community. Just as a virus introduced into the bloodstream will permeate and vitiate the entire organism until the body sets up resistance, so in the Society of Friends schismatic movements starting on one side of the Atlantic quickly spread to the other, revealing unmistakably the interrelatedness of its widely separated parts.

I shall refer briefly in conclusion to two of these schisms—that of John Perrot, which originated in England and spread to the colonies, and that of George Keith, which started in Pennsylvania and was carried to Great Britain.[40] There is no need to go into the theological bases of these movements. Suffice it to say that Perrot's heresy was an individualistic, almost solipsistic mysticism which denied all outward arrangements in worship, including even the custom of removing the hat as a mark of respect to the Deity when another Friend was praying; and that Keith's was an attack on the Quaker belief that men were saved by the inward Christ "without anything else," that is, without need of faith in the historic Christ or the Scriptures.

The "hat" heresy, which sprang up in England in 1661, was carried by Perrot himself to the West Indies and thence to Virginia and Maryland; its effects were ultimately felt as far north as New York and, on the other side of the Atlantic world, at Rotterdam.[41] George Fox had to discharge several epistolary broadsides, and visiting ministers like John Burnyeat had to labor mightily, before the Perrot faction in America was quelled. But within a comparatively few years what Fox called the "spirit that run into the hat" was completely exorcised, and peace was restored to the church.[42]

The Keithian schism, which arose in the 1690's, showed that transatlantic currents of heretical thought could flow in the opposite direction.[43] Keith's followers, who called themselves "Christian Quakers," may have well included as many as a quarter of the Pennsylvania and New Jersey Friends. The heresiarch was duly censured and finally disowned by Philadelphia Yearly Meeting in 1692. This action was followed by judgments given against him by Friends in Barbados, Virginia, Maryland, New Jersey, Long Island, and Rhode Island—a striking instance in itself of the scope and effectiveness of the Quaker community.[44] Keith then carried his case to London where a group of "Christian Quakers" soon sprang into existence and where in 1695 he was again disowned. By the turn of the century Philadelphia Friends were able to report that "our old adversaries formerly Seduced and Headed by George Keith, are almost Mouldered to Nothing."[45] Community was restored.

Such was the structure and such the functioning of the Atlantic Quaker community in the seventeenth century. "By the opening of the eighteenth century," observed the late Rufus M. Jones with characteristic insight, "the Friends were *one* people throughout the world, though there was absolutely no *bond* but love and fellowship. There was no visible head to the Society, no official creed, no ecclesiastical body which held sway and authority. But instead of being an aggregation of separated units, the Society was in an extraordinary sense *a living group*."[46]

CHAPTER III

Quakerism and Politics

Faith in the Inward Light implied equality among men, for God, so the early Quakers believed, had bestowed His Spirit impartially upon all His children. It also implied the rejection of all violence and fighting, for he who would "mind the Light" would be brought, as George Fox was, to live "in the virtue of that life and power that took away the occasion of all wars"; he would come into "the covenant of peace, which was before wars and strifes were."[1] The use of the "plain language" of *thee* and *thou*, the refusal to doff the hat and bow low before social superiors, were early practical expressions of the religious testimony for equality. The concern for racial equality, whether in the United States or in South Africa, is its outstanding present-day manifestation. Conscientious objection to military service was, and still is, an important Quaker witness for peace. Almost from the beginning, however, it has been supplemented by positive efforts to promote amicable relationships among the nations of the world.[2]

But equality and peace are not merely religious concepts with implications only for private conduct. They are political principles to which statesmen in the modern world almost universally give their adherence, or at least lip service, when they insist that their governments are "democratic" and "peace-loving." From the beginning of the Quaker movement, some Friends have felt impelled to go into politics in order to strike down artificial obstacles to human equality and eliminate the causes of war. But their path has been a peculiarly difficult one. For politics inevitably involves the manipulation of power, which is foreign to the Quaker way. And to be successful in politics—which is accurately defined as "the art of the possible"—one must be adept at compromise, which is contrary to the Quaker insistence on fidelity to a perfectionist ethic.

36

So almost invariably when the Quaker has sought to translate his religious ideals into political reality, he has found himself in a dilemma. Shall he remain intransigently faithful to his ideal and forfeit the chance of immediate success? Or shall he give way a little, relax his perfectionist demands, and score at least a partial victory for his cause? Sometimes he finds himself in the impossible situation of the antislavery Friends in the American Civil War, whose plight was perceptively described by Abraham Lincoln: "On principle and faith, opposed to both war and oppression, they can only practically oppose oppression by war. In this hard dilemma," Lincoln went on, "some have chosen one horn and some the other."[3] So it has nearly always been when Friends have confronted their culture in the role of the politician: some have deliberately kept to the path of participation at the partial sacrifice of their ideals, and some have chosen the path of renunciation with a consequent loss of immediate impact on history.

There is a third path, however, which avoids compromise on the one hand and indifferentism on the other. It is perhaps the distinctive Quaker way in relation to politics, but it too is strewn with formidable difficulties. From the very beginning some Friends have felt a religious concern in times of crisis to confront the heads of government directly, in the manner of the Hebrew prophets, with the radical demands of the Christian ethic, divorced from all considerations of expediency or policy. Today the Friends Committee on National Legislation in Washington seeks to represent this Quaker approach to politics by keeping Friends alert to the moral implications of pending legislation and encouraging them to lay their religious concerns before their Congressmen; and an international "Quaker team" labors unobtrusively but persistently at United Nations headquarters in New York to keep alive the conviction that genuine peace, which is God's will for the nations, is still a real option in diplomacy. But the Quaker who presumes to take the prophetic stance before the rulers of this world, if he is to avoid mere busybodyism, must earn the right by a consistent life of devotion to the absolute standards of the New Testament and sensitiveness to the leadings of the Inward Light.

1

In October, 1656, George Fox had a memorable interview with Oliver Cromwell, Lord Protector of England. It was one of the great moments of a great century, for here, face to face, were two of the most powerful personalities of the age, the one the military dictator of the British Isles at the pinnacle of his worldly power, the other a crude, rustic preacher who had just spent eight months in one of England's foulest prisons. They met in Whitehall, at the very heart of the British government. Fox bluntly took the Protector to task for persecuting Friends when he should have protected them. Then, characteristically, he set about trying to make a Quaker out of Cromwell, to turn him to "the light of Christ who had enlightened every man that cometh into the world." Cromwell, in an argumentative mood, took issue with Fox's theology, but Fox had no patience with his objections. "The power of the Lord God riz in me," he wrote, "and I was moved to bid him lay down his crown at the feet of Jesus."[4]

Cromwell knew what Fox meant, for two years earlier he had received a strange and disturbing missive in which he had read these words:

God is my witness, by whom I am moved to give this forth for the Truth's sake, from him whom the world calls George Fox; who is the son of God who is sent to stand a witness against all violence and against all the works of darkness, and to turn people from the darkness to the light, and to bring them from the occasion of the war and from the occasion of the magistrate's sword. . . .[5]

The man who persisted in calling himself the "son of God"—he later acknowledged that he had many brothers—was demanding nothing less than that the military ruler of all England should forthwith disavow all violence and all coercion, make Christ's law of love the supreme law of the land, and substitute the mild dictates of the Sermon on the Mount for the Instrument of Government by which he ruled. In a word, Fox would have him make England a kind of pilot project for the Kingdom of Heaven. Fox was a revolutionary. He had no patience with the relativities and compromises of political life. His testimony was an uncompromising testimony for the radical Christian ethic of love and nonviolence, and he would apply it in the arena of politics as in every other sphere of life. It is not recorded that Cromwell took his advice. Neither is it recorded that Fox ever receded an inch from his radical perfectionism. The absolute demands he made upon Cromwell three hundred years ago may stand as one pole of Quaker thought on politics.

It was just one hundred years later, in October, 1756, that the Quakers abdicated their political control of Pennsylvania, and the "Holy Experiment" in government in the Valley of the Delaware came to a close. For three-quarters of a century, first in West New Jersey, then in Pennsylvania, Friends had been deeply involved in the day-to-day business of politics—winning elections, administering local and provincial government, struggling for power among themselves, contending with non-Quaker politicians, squabbling with neighboring provinces, wrangling with the imperial authorities in Whitehall. Though William Penn had founded his Quaker utopia by the Delaware on the proposition that government was "a part of religion itself, a thing sacred in its institution and end," neither he nor his successors had pretended to maintain George Fox's absolute witness.

As office-seekers they had often fallen short of perfect Christian charity in their relations with their opponents. As officeholders they had often found it necessary to compromise their highest principles in order to stay in office. As judges they had sentenced men to death. As legislators within the British Empire they had appropriated funds with which the Crown had carried on its wars with France and Spain. In some degree every one of them had come to terms with the world, had compromised the purity of his religious testimony as a Quaker. But they had created in the American wilderness a commonwealth in which civil and religious liberty, social and political equality, domestic and external peace had reigned to a degree and for a length of time unexampled in the history of the Western world. When the Quaker lawmakers of Pennsylvania stepped down and gave the province into the hands of "the world's people," something went out of American political life—something that we have been two hundred years trying to restore. The relative testimony of the colonial Pennsylvania politicians may stand as the other pole of political thought and practice in the Society of Friends.

Between these two poles Quaker political attitudes and behavior have oscillated, and the main purpose of this essay is to trace historically the path of that oscillation, to underline some of the dilemmas in which Friends have found themselves in relation to politics, and, if possible, to draw from the record some conclusions which may have contemporary relevance.

2

We must begin by recognizing how thoroughly primitive Quakerism shared the spirit of millennial hope, the exhilarating atmosphere of expectancy that marked the middle years of the seventeenth century. It was a period, like the early years of the Christian Church itself, when many religious people in England looked for the imminent return of Christ on the clouds of glory and the prompt establishment of the Kingdom of Heaven on earth. It was the period of the Barebones Parliament, that curious collection of assorted fanatics who hoped to usher in the Rule of the Saints in England. It was the period of the Fifth Monarchy Men, those violent zealots who planned to enthrone King Jesus in succession to the late Charles I. The apocalyptic imagery of the Books of Daniel and Revelation worked like yeast in English minds, and the radical ethics of the New Testament were spawning visionary schemes for the root-and-branch reform of English society. The Quaker movement, we must recall, grew out of the same Puritan soil as these other manifestations of left-wing Protestantism; its early leaders shared fully in the apocalyptic excitement, the zeal for social reform, the identification of politics with religion.[6]

"Laws and decrees shall be changed and renewed," exulted Edward Burrough. "Every yoke and burden shall be taken off from the neck of the poor; true judgment and justice, mercy and truth, peace and righteousness shall be exalted; and all the nations shall have judges as at the first and counselors as at the beginning."[7] When George Fox "was moved to sound the day of the Lord" from the top of Pendle Hill, he was not behaving exactly like a twentieth century Philadelphia Quaker, but he was acting quite in the spirit of the time.[8] And when William Tomlinson cried out: "Woe, woe, woe, to the oppressors of the earth, who grind the faces of the poor," and warned that "God will in time hear the groanings of the whole creation, and then, woe, woe, woe, to you who have been such oppressors and hard-hearted taskmasters," he was speaking in the authentic vein of prophetic Christianity and adding one more Quaker voice to the chorus of social protest that reached a crescendo in England at the end of the 1650's.

It is now pretty clear, despite the reticence of Quaker literature on the subject, that in the critical year 1659, just before the Restoration of Charles II, the Rump Parliament made a remarkable proposal to the Quakers—"nothing less than that they should aid in a sweeping reorganization of . . . the Commonwealth government—a reorganization in which justiceships would be given to Friends or to others sympathetic to the Quaker movement."[9] What is more, many Quakers were prepared to rise to the challenge and take their part in administering the Holy Commonwealth. Friends in Somersetshire described themselves as "ready (for Truth's sake) to serve the commonwealth to the uttermost of their ability," and it seems probable that five Friends in Westminster and seven in Bristol were actually appointed commissioners of the militia. The French ambassador wrote home that the hard-pressed government was relying for its support on the Quakers: "The Spirit of God, by which they are ruled," he reported, "now permits them to take part in the affairs of this world, and the Parliament seems inclined to make use of them."

We are accustomed to thinking that the early Friends stood aloof from politics, and we find it hard to see how men who had renounced force could justify administering the militia. Yet given the apocalyptic atmosphere of the time, it is not impossible to understand how Friends could have agreed to accept public office, even to take up the magistrate's sword, in the interests of establishing the Rule of the Saints. For once the regime of the righteous was set up, all swords would, no doubt, be turned into plowshares and all spears into pruning hooks. After all, one of the earliest epistles of advice to Friends, the ancestor of all Quaker books of discipline, a remarkable letter sent out from Balby in Yorkshire in 1656, had recommended "that if any be called to serve the Commonwealth in any public service, which is for the public wealth and good, that with cheerfulness it be undertaken, and in faithfulness discharged unto God: that therein patterns and examples in the thing that is righteous, they may be, to those that be without."[10]

But the revolution of the Saints did not come off. Instead the unsaintly Charles II was restored to the throne in 1660, and Puritan apocalypticism fizzled out in the absurd and abortive little rising of the Fifth Monarchy Men in January, 1661. If George Fox had ever really favored Quaker participation in the politics of the Saints, he had had by now some sober second thoughts; some scholars think the ten-week-long "time of darkness" into which he was plunged in the middle of 1659 was a time of inward struggle over this very issue. In any case, by the end of that year he was advising Friends everywhere to "keep out of the powers of the earth that run into wars and fightings" and to "take heed of joining with this or the other, or meddling with any, or being busy with other men's matters; but mind the Lord, and his power and his service."[11] After the fiasco of the Fifth Monarchy rising, innocent Friends were taken up by the hundreds and imprisoned on charges of conspiracy to overthrow the government—charges based on a doctrine of "guilt by association" as far-fetched and vicious as that which has flourished in our own day. To clear themselves of suspicion a number of leading Friends, including Fox, issued a public declaration that they had never been concerned in any plots for the violent overthrow of the government, that indeed the Spirit of Truth would never lead them to "fight and war against any man with outward weapons, neither for the kingdom of Christ, nor for the kingdoms of this world."[12]

3

The traumatic experiences of the Restoration year had a lasting effect on the Quaker attitude toward politics. Many Friends reacted sharply against anything that smacked of partisan politics and took the position that a Quaker should have nothing to do with the affairs of this world, that his citizenship was in another Kingdom. The words of Alexander Parker in 1660 are representative of this attitude: "My advice and counsel," he wrote, "is, that every one of you, who love and believe in the Light, be still and quiet, and side not with any parties; but own and cherish the good wherever it appears, and testify against the evil. . . ."[13]

This attitude of aloofness and neutrality was the dominant one in the Society of Friends during the fifteen years following the Restoration. All the strength the Society could muster was required simply to survive, to weather the storm of persecution that Charles

II loosed upon them. But political interests were not dead. Around the year 1675 some Friends at least began to show a new concern for politics. There was no dream of capturing England for the Kingdom of God now. The House of Stuart was too strongly entrenched. Moreover, Quakers were excluded from office by the requirement of an oath, which they could not in conscience take. And anyhow, the confident millennial mood of midcentury had passed forever. But Friends had meanwhile strengthened their own internal government by creating a network of Monthly Meetings all over the country with appropriate central agencies in London. Consequently, they now had the means of bringing their organized influence to bear on the British government at one limited but—to them—all-important point: religious toleration. Quaker action to bring an end to the persecution took two forms: on the one hand, an attempt to influence elections, and, on the other, an effort to influence legislation. In other words, Friends engaged in a certain amount of electioneering and lobbying.

In 1675, for example, the Second-Day Morning Meeting in London encouraged Friends to vote only for Parliament men who would sign an agreement to work for toleration. Six years later, the Meeting for Sufferings was urging Quakers who had the franchise to vote for "sober, discreet, and moderate men . . . that are against persecution and Popery, and that deport themselves tenderly towards our Friends."[14] William Penn was, of course, the most active political Quaker of the time. Everyone knows about his "Holy Experiment" in Pennsylvania (to which I will come back presently), but before he set that experiment on foot he had a fling at politics in England. Though he had announced, just a few years before, that "it is not our business to meddle with government," he took to the hustings twice— in 1677 and 1679—in a vain effort to elect his friend Algernon Sidney to Parliament—Sidney who dreamed of transforming King Charles's England into a republic. Friends were clearly a political bloc to be reckoned with in those years. So active were they in the Parliamentary elections that the King's friends actually promised Penn to free his people from persecution if he would pledge their political support or at least their neutrality.[15] And it has been plausibly argued that King Charles's willingness to grant Penn a huge province across the sea was dictated by the hope of draining off to America a troublesome portion of his political opposition.[16]

But in the long run lobbying was for Friends a more congenial method of influencing politics than electioneering. Quakers had been engaged in lobbying—that is to say, in seeking to influence legislators by personal visits—ever since 1659, when 165 Friends went to Westminster Hall and sent into the House of Commons a paper offering to lie "body for body" in jail in place of their imprisoned and suffering fellow Quakers.[17] But after 1675 they intensified their legislative activity, seeking acts for the release of prisoners and the ending of persecution. The Meeting for Sufferings coordinated the work. The weightiest Friends in England, including George Fox and William Penn, busied themselves buttonholing Members of Parliament and appearing at committee hearings. The Yearly Meeting even rented a room in a coffeehouse hard by the Houses of Parliament for a headquarters.[18] An unfriendly observer noted sourly that "it was indeed somewhat scandalous, to see, when any Bill or Petition was defending, wherein the Quakers had their Account or Design, what crowding, what soliciting, what treating and trading there was by that sly and artificial set of Men. . . ." And another critic observed that "Their broad Hatts, their short Crevatts, their dour Looks, [and] Subtil Carriages" were always in evidence when the House of Commons was in session.[19] The legislative struggle for religious liberty was substantially won in 1689 with the passage of the great Toleration Act, but the lobbying efforts went on, until Friends were finally granted the right to substitute a simple affirmation for a formal oath in 1722. From time to time in the course of this campaign the Meeting for Sufferings urged Friends to write their Parliament men on the subject.[20] If anyone thinks the techniques of the Friends Committee on National Legislation, the Quaker lobby in Washington, are a modern innovation, he knows little of Quaker history.

4

The Affirmation Act of 1722 finally gave English Quakers many of the privileges of citizenship they had hitherto lacked, including the right to sue in court and to vote without impediment (though not to hold public office). Curiously enough, the achievement of most of the privileges of citizenship was followed by a widespread disinclination to exercise them. Friends in England—I am leaving the

American story to one side for the moment—were entering the age of Quietism. The feeling grew that a good Quaker should have as little as possible to do with earthly government, that he must avoid the temptations, the distractions, the compromises, the corruptions of political life, that he ought to maintain his religious testimonies with absolute purity, in isolation, if need be, from the life of his time. He must be—it was a favorite phrase of the period—among "the quiet in the land."

We saw this attitude taking root among the English Friends at the time of the Restoration in 1660; in the eighteenth century it became almost a dogma. Listen to Samuel Scott, a fairly typical "public Friend," on the Parliamentary elections of 1780:

The parliament being dissolved, a general election is coming on; the devil cometh forth, and hell from beneath. . . . it becometh not the members of our society to meddle much in those matters, or to be active in political disquisitions. . . . In respect to elections, we ought to go no farther than voting for the candidates we best approve, and declaring our preference of them, without endeavouring by any other means to influence others. "Israel is to dwell alone, and not to be mixed with the people."[21]

Some Friends even counseled against voting. Here is the advice of Thomas Shillitoe, an extreme Quietist, in 1820: "Friends, let us dare not meddle with political matters. . . . Endeavour to keep that ear closed, which will be itching to hear the news of the day and what is going forward in the political circles." Friends, he thought, should be resolutely oblivious to the world around them. "Avoid reading political publications," he warned, "and, as much as possible, newspapers."[22] The religion of these Quietist Friends was a tender plant that must be carefully guarded against blighting contact with "the world."

5

The climate of English Quaker opinion on politics did not change until well into the nineteenth century. After the passage of the great Reform Bill of 1832 it became possible at last for Friends to qualify for Parliament by taking an affirmation in place of an oath. The first Quaker to take a seat in the House of Commons was Joseph Pease, who was elected in 1833, though his father, his mother-in-law, and his Monthly Meeting all tried to dissuade him from entering the hurly-burly of public life. He sat in the House for several years, always wearing his plain Quaker coat, steadfastly declining, in Quaker fashion, to use formal titles of address even in Parliament.

Ten years after Joseph Pease broke the ice, a Quaker statesman greater than he—indeed one of the towering figures in nineteenth century British politics—entered Parliament. I shall not recount the story of John Bright's career or attempt to catalogue all his achievements. I shall simply mention some of the liberal causes for which he struggled nobly and, in the main, successfully: the abolition of compulsory church rates or tithes, against which Friends had long borne a testimony; the repeal of the Corn Laws, which were taking bread out of the mouths of the poor; the extension of the franchise, which had hitherto been denied to many poorer folk in town and country; the emancipation of the Jews, who had been subject to civil disabilities based on prejudice; the abolition of capital punishment, still a subject of political debate in England; justice and fair treatment for the people of Ireland and India, who in different ways were suffering from oppression; steadfast opposition to the Crimean War, a war which modern historians unite in condemning as unjust and unnecessary; the humanitarian protest against the wanton bombarding of Alexandria in 1882, the issue over which he resigned from Gladstone's cabinet. Every one of these causes was in harmony with his humane and pacifist impulses as a Quaker. William E. Gladstone was not merely indulging in the conventions of funeral eulogy when he said of Bright "that he elevated political life to a higher elevation, and to a loftier standard, and that he . . . thereby bequeathed to his country the character of a statesman which can be made the subject not only of admiration, and not only of gratitude, but of reverential contemplation."[23]

Yet John Bright himself would have been the first to admit that he had not been a completely "consistent" Friend throughout his long career in politics, that the testimonies of his religious society were counsels of perfection which a practical politician could not uphold in all their purity. He had, for instance, approved the bloody suppression of the Indian Mutiny of 1857. He had been a warm supporter of the North in our fratricidal Civil War, writing to John Greenleaf Whittier that "war was and is the only way out of the desperate difficulty of your country," and to another correspondent that "I want no end of the war, and no compromise, and no reunion till the Negro is made free beyond all chance of failure."[24] And in his social philosophy he was so much the captive of the *laissez faire* doctrines of his time as to oppose every effort to limit by law the number of hours women should work in factories.[25] In other words, one cannot overlook the plain fact that Bright's contributions as a Quaker statesman, notable as they were, were achieved at the sacrifice of consistency as a Quaker.

Since John Bright's time there has been an unbroken tradition of political Quakerism in England. More than sixty Friends have held seats in Parliament—and they have held them right through two world wars. Scores, probably hundreds more have served on county councils and in other posts in local government.

Meanwhile the official attitude of London Yearly Meeting has changed slowly from one of reluctant acquiescence to one of wholehearted endorsement of political activity. The London Discipline of 1861 took pains to point out some of the duties of public office that would be inconsistent with Quaker principles—administering oaths, enforcing ecclesiastical demands, calling out the armed forces—and warned Friends to consider seriously "whether it is right for them to accept an office which involves such alternatives." Furthermore, the Discipline went on, still under the sway of the Quietist fear of "the world": "When we consider the seductive influence of popularity, and the self-satisfaction consequent upon the successful efforts of the intellectual powers, even in a good cause, we feel bound with affectionate earnestness, to caution our friends against being led to take an undue part in the many exciting objects of the day."[26] By the beginning of the twentieth century, however, the Yearly Meeting was offering advice in quite a different vein. "The free institutions under which we live," read the Discipline of 1911, "give many of our members a direct share in the responsibilities of government, and in forming the healthy public opinion that will lead to purity of administration and righteousness of policy. This responsibility belongs to them by virtue of their citizenship, and our members can no more rightly remain indifferent to it, than to the duties which they owe to their parents and near relatives." "In view of the opportunities for public service opened to Friends during the last half century," it went on, "we desire to press upon them the duty of qualifying themselves, so that they may be 'prepared unto every good work.' "[27] The change from the cautious spirit of the Yearly Meeting's advice just half a century before is too striking to miss.

The most critical test of any Quaker's devotion to his traditional religious testimonies comes in wartime, and this is especially true for the Quaker in public office. A student at Swarthmore College tabulated the votes of the Quaker Members of Parliament on crucial measures during the two world wars. She found about what one might expect: that some were consistent pacifist Quakers throughout, voting for no military measures and vigorously defending the rights of conscientious objectors; that some were pretty consistently unpacifist and un-Quakerly in their attitude, supporting nearly all the war government's measures; and that some were simply not consistent (that is, on some issues they voted their Quaker consciences and on others they did not). From her analysis she concluded that it is not inherently impossible to be a consistent Quaker pacifist in government, even in wartime: here the notable career of the late T. Edmund Harvey, who sat in Parliament during both world wars, was her chief exhibit. On the other hand, she was obliged to grant that if one is to avoid mere negativism and obstructionism, it is often necessary to be silent and therefore, to a degree, uninfluential with respect to most major issues, and to concentrate one's efforts on such minor though important problems as securing fair treatment for CO's.[28] The experience of the English Quaker M.P.'s suggests that the path of a religious idealist in practical politics is not an easy one.

6

So far I have focused on the relationship of English Quakers to politics. I can deal with the American experience more briefly, though it is far from a simple story. The elements are the same, but the historical development of attitudes is curiously different; in fact, the American experience reverses the British to produce a kind of historical counterpoint. For Quakers on this side of the Atlantic were becoming more and more deeply involved in politics just when their British cousins were detaching themselves from it; later, American Friends reacted toward Quietism and noninvolvement as the English moved away from that attitude and began to take an active part in government.

There were four American colonies in which, for longer or shorter periods, the powers of government were in Quaker hands. In Rhode Island between 1672 and 1768 ten Quakers served for a total of thirty years as governors, and other Friends held office as deputy-governors and assemblymen. West New Jersey, especially during its first quarter-century, from 1674 to 1702, was in every sense a Quaker colony. Everyone knows that Pennsylvania was controlled by Friends from its founding in 1682 down to the middle of the eighteenth century. And for a brief period the Carolinas were governed by an able Quaker administrator, John Archdale. Obviously there are plenty of materials here for the study of Quaker experience in government, and they are far from having been exhausted by historians. I shall limit myself to one point, the same point I discussed in connection with John Bright and the other Quaker M.P.'s—the inevitability of compromise. I shall draw my illustrations from what is usually, and rightly, considered the most successful Quaker experience in government—William Penn's "Holy Experiment" in colonial Pennsylvania.

As a concerned Friend William Penn gave his allegiance to the fundamental principle of Christian pacifism. So, as individual Friends, did most of his associates and successors who dominated Pennsylvania politics for three-quarters of a century. But as responsible legislators and administrators governing a constituent part of the British Empire, they found it impossible in practice to maintain that principle without abatement or compromise.

Compromise indeed was built into the very foundations of the "Holy Experiment": by his charter from King Charles II Penn was given power "to levy, muster, and train all sorts of men . . . and to make war and pursue the enemies and . . . put them to death by the law of war . . . and do all and every act which to the charge and office of a captain-general of an army belongeth." In other words, his authority, like that of the President of the United States, included the powers of Commander in Chief of the army and navy. Penn apparently had no scruples about accepting this authority, which was an essential condition of his receiving the colony for his "Holy Experiment." No doubt he believed there would be no need to exercise it in a Quaker commonwealth. But events and the logic of Pennsyl-

vania's status in the British Empire showed otherwise. When Britain
went to war with France or Spain, as she did four times during the
next seventy-five years, orders came from London to put the colony
in a posture of military defense and to contribute funds for the prosecution of the war. The Quaker rulers of Pennsylvania knew they might
lose control of the colony and be forced to abandon their "Holy Experiment" if they did not comply. They grew adept at the politics of
shuffle and evasion, but in the end they usually found ways to meet
the military demands. The usual formula was to grant money "for
the Queen's use." No one was deceived as to the use the Queen
would make of the money. But, as one of the leading Quaker politicians put it, "We did not see it to be inconsistent with our principles
to give the Queen money notwithstanding any use she might put it
to, that being not our part but hers."

Presently, the legislative dodges became more ingenious. During
King George's War the Quaker Assembly voted four thousand pounds
for the purchase of "bread, beef, pork, flour, wheat and other grains";
and when the governor interpreted "other grains" to mean gun-
powder, no Quaker legislator is known to have objected. By 1755 the
Assembly was appropriating as much as fifty thousand pounds—a
huge sum considering the time and place—"for the King's use." In
the following year Pennsylvania found itself actually at war with the
Delaware and Shawnee Indians. By now the time for shuffling and
evasion was past: Quakers simply could not administer a province at
war. And so the majority of the Friends stepped down from office and
the "Holy Experiment" was over.

I have stressed this single point of compromise with the peace
testimony—and I could have shown it in other areas as well—not to
pass judgment on the political Quakers of Pennsylvania. They had a
noble and forward-looking experiment in government committed to
their hands. I am not disposed to blame them for wanting to preserve
the substance of that experiment as long as they could, even at some
cost in terms of consistency with principle. I merely wish us to be
clear that even in William Penn's Quaker utopia the exercise of
political power involved compromise, involved some abatement of
Quaker ideals.[29]

In 1758, two years after the Quaker abdication in Pennsylvania,
Philadelphia Yearly Meeting advised its members to "beware of ac-

cepting of, or continuing in, the exercise of any office or station in civil society or government" which required actions inconsistent with Quaker testimonies. The pendulum had swung sharply away from political activity, and I think it is fair to say that American Friends have tended almost from that day to this to avoid direct participation in politics, at least in the sense of seeking elective office. The strong feelings of North Carolina Friends on this subject a hundred years ago are reflected in the unequivocal language of the Yearly Meeting Discipline of 1854: "It is the sense of the Yearly Meeting, that if any of our members accept, or act in, the office of member of the federal or state legislature, justice of the peace, clerk of a court, coroner, sheriff, or constable, that they be dealt with, and if they cannot be convinced of the inconsistency of their conduct, after sufficient labor, they be disowned."[30] Philadelphia's attitude, a century or more ago, was only a little less sweeping: Friends were advised under pain of disownment "to decline the acceptance of any office or station in civil government, the duties of which are inconsistent with our religious principles"; furthermore they were urged not "to be active or accessory in electing or promoting to be elected, their brethren to such offices or stations in civil government."[31] Quietism in relation to politics had become the rule among American Friends just as British Friends were beginning to break away from it.

In recent years the official attitude of many American Yearly Meetings has swung over to a position not unlike that of London Yearly Meeting, though this shift was neither prompted nor followed, as in England, by any significant migration of American Quakers into public office. In 1927 Philadelphia Yearly Meeting declared its belief that "the Kingdom of God on earth is advanced by those who devote themselves with unselfish public spirit to the building of a high national character, and to the shaping of a righteous policy of government both at home and abroad." It urged Friends "to be active in the performance of all the duties of good citizenship," and defined the duties of good citizenship specifically to include officeholding.[32] In 1945 the Five Years Meeting, representing the great majority of American Quakers, offered similar advice: "It behooves all Friends," read its Discipline, "to fit themselves for efficient public service and to be faithful to their performance of duty as they are gifted and guided by the inspiration of God."[33]

The book of *Faith and Practice* issued by the reunited Philadelphia Yearly Meeting in 1955, repeats the earlier advice about accepting office when summoned to it, but adds a cautionary proviso: "Necessity for group action," it suggests, "may, however, present difficult problems for the office holder who seeks to be single-minded in his loyalty to God. A prayerful search," it goes on in slightly cryptic language, "may lead to a suitable adjustment which need not establish a precedent but should be kept before the Father in Heaven for further light." But, "It may become necessary," the statement concludes, "to sacrifice position to conscience and expediency to principle."[34]

7

This sober advice calls to mind a wise passage from Rufus Jones:

There has always been in the Society of Friends a group of persons pledged unswervingly to the ideal. To those who form this inner group compromise is under no circumstance allowable. If there comes a collision between allegiance to the ideal and the holding of public office, then the office must be deserted. If obedience to the soul's vision involves eye or hand, houses or lands or life, they must be immediately surrendered. But there has always been as well another group who have held it to be equally imperative to work out their principles of life in the complex affairs of the community and the state, where to gain an end one must yield something; where to get on one must submit to existing conditions; and where to achieve ultimate triumph one must risk his ideals to the tender mercies of a world not yet ripe for them.[35]

If anything is clear from our quick historical survey, I think it must be this: that there is no one Quaker attitude toward politics. Historically, Quakers can be found practicing and preaching almost every possible position from full participation to complete withdrawal and abstention. Rufus Jones has isolated for us, in the passage I just quoted, the two polar extremes. I would underline the dilemma implicit in his description. If a concerned Quaker (or any man or woman committed to an absolute religious ethic) decides to enter practical politics in order to translate his principles into actuality, he may achieve a relative success: he may be able to raise the level of political life in his time, as John Bright did, or maintain a comparatively happy and just and peaceful society, as the Quaker legislators of Pennsylvania did. But he can apparently do it only at a price—the price of compromise, of the partial betrayal of his ideals. If, on the other hand, he decides to preserve his ideals intact, to maintain his religious testimonies unsullied and pure, he may be able to do that, but again at a price—the price of isolation, of withdrawal from the main stream of life in his time, of renouncing the opportunity directly and immediately to influence history.

Let me call the two positions the relativist and the absolutist. And let me suggest that perhaps each one needs the other. The relativist needs the absolutist to keep alive and clear the vision of the City of God while he struggles in some measure to realize it in the City of Earth. And, conversely, the absolutist needs the relativist, lest the vision remain the possession of a few only, untranslated into any degree of reality for the world as a whole. Which position an individual Friend will take will depend, I suppose, on his temperament. For those who incline toward the more absolutist position, there is wisdom in the statement of Henry Hodgkin, an English Friend: "With my conception of the Christian life," he wrote,

I do not see that it would be possible for me to enter the world of politics as it is at present run. For example, anyone who wants to make his influence felt must be allied to a party and accept many compromises. He must use methods current in politics but, to say the least, highly distasteful to a moral man. . . . Time was when I felt that for anyone to embark on such a career was a comedown from the highest level of Christian living. While I am as far as ever from being able to go into politics myself, I should now hold that God may be just as truly revealed in a person who enters this field and accepts conditions which I could not accept as, let us say, a devoted evangelist.[36]

Of course, neither of these two polar positions is uniquely Quaker. The Mennonites in their quiet way have practiced the absolutist withdrawal from the world longer and more consistently than Friends have ever done. And many religious idealists have gone into politics at some sacrifice of their ideals to work for a relatively better world. I should like to suggest in closing that if there is any distinctive Quaker posture vis à vis politics, it is one which I might describe as the prophetic stance or the role of the divine lobbyist. By this I do not mean approaching legislators for favors—though Friends have sometimes done that, as in the case of the Affirmation Act. I am think-

ing rather of George Fox in 1656 bidding Oliver Cromwell to lay
down his crown at the feet of Jesus, of Robert Barclay in 1679 standing
before the representatives of the European powers at Nimwegen
and calling upon them to settle a peace upon Christian principles, or
Joseph Sturge in 1855 pleading with Tsar Alexander II for reconcilia-
tion with England, of Rufus Jones in 1938 interceding for the Jews
before the chiefs of the Gestapo, or any Friend visiting his congress-
man with a religious concern. All these, like the prophets of Israel,
have felt a divine call to "speak Truth to power," to lay a concern
upon those who are charged with the governing of men.[37] The Friends
Committee on National Legislation is, in a sense, an institutionaliza-
tion of this age-old Quaker practice.

There are grave perils and responsibilities in this role. There is the
peril of hiding a selfish motive behind a façade of religious concern:
a Quaker lobby must never fall to the level of the lumber lobby or
the oil lobby. There is the peril of mistaking a personal impulse, no
matter how altruistic, for a divine call, of becoming a mere busybody,
troubling harassed legislators with trivial or irresponsible demands.
And there is the responsibility of "earning the right" by a consistent
pattern of religious dedication and service to speak to those who bear
the heavy burden of political power. This kind of prophetic mission
to the rulers of men is a distinctively Quaker approach to politics.
When carried out under a deep religious concern by a person whose
own life speaks of a genuine commitment to a spiritual vision, such
an approach can be a way of avoiding the dilemma of isolation on
the one hand and compromise on the other, a way of combining consistency of life with relevance to history. Like the prophet Zechariah
before his king, Friends can still pronounce the timeless but always
timely message: "Not by might, nor by power, but by my spirit, saith
the Lord."[38]

CHAPTER IV

Quakerism, Capitalism, and Science

I. THE QUAKER ETHIC AND THE SPIRIT OF CAPITALISM

The Quaker approach to our culture on its economic side has been curiously ambivalent. On the one hand, the strong sense of community has expressed itself in the practice of mutual aid within the household of the faith, in unstinting service to suffering humanity anywhere in the world, and in sporadic but sharp criticism of the acquisitive spirit. On the other hand, the leaven of individualism, working in the economic sphere, has promoted an attitude remarkably conducive to success in our competitive business system.

The popular conception of the Quaker for three centuries has reflected both aspects of his social and economic ethic. Friends have long been known as simple, warmhearted angels of mercy, compassionate, generous, self-forgetful to a fault. But alongside this favorable image in the folk imagination, like a photographic negative, stands the contrary impression of the canny, tight-fisted, prosperous Quaker trader, a figure of fun in many a ballad and jest. Today the average American's mental picture of the Quaker, if it is not limited to the effigy on the Quaker Oats box, is probably compounded of his awareness of the world-wide humanitarian work of the American Friends Service Committee and his memory of old jokes about the Philadelphia Friends as a "God-fearing, money-making people." The popular impression has accurately mirrored the latent conflict in the Quaker approach to culture in its economic aspect. As Kenneth Boulding, a Quaker economist, has said, "It is the tension between the Quaker ethic pulling toward collectivism and the Quaker religion pulling toward individualism which explains the wide divergence of attitudes within the Society on this matter."[1]

A great deal has been written about the Quaker humanitarians and social critics—about the early social reformer John Bellers, whom Karl Marx called "a veritable phenomenon in the history of political economy"; about John Woolman and Anthony Benezet, who trenchantly criticized the materialism of their contemporaries (including some of their Quaker contemporaries); about Lucretia Mott, John Greenleaf Whittier, Elizabeth Fry, and other Quaker reformers who labored to rectify the abuses of nineteenth century society. We are much less well acquainted with the Quaker bankers of the City of London and the Quaker merchants of colonial America—with Abraham Darby, the English ironmaster who revolutionized the iron industry; with William Rotch of Nantucket who developed the romantic quest of the whale into a highly organized business; with Moses Brown, in whose textile mill the Industrial Revolution was domesticated in the United States; with Edward Pease, whose financial support enabled George Stephenson to build the first successful railroad. To quote Kenneth Boulding again: "It is clear that Friends have been deeply implicated in the rise of the whole set of institutional and technical changes, which go under the name of 'capitalism'. . . ."[2]

The philosophy of economic individualism which underlies modern capitalism has obviously been a primary motive force in Western society. The following essay describes some of the Quaker attitudes which fed that philosophy in its formative period. The story it tells is a small but not unimportant chapter in the history of the contribution of the "Protestant ethic" to the "spirit of capitalism." It makes no pretense to exhaust the subject. It focuses on a particular group of Quaker businessmen—the merchants who set the tone of economic thought and practice in Benjamin Franklin's Philadelphia.

The complete story of the Quaker economic ethic would take full account of the countervailing impulse toward brotherhood, social justice, and community responsibility.[3] Properly told, that story might point the way to a resolution of one of the basic conflicts in modern culture. For, as a group of distinguished theologians reported to the World Council of Churches in 1948, the old dilemma of social responsibility versus individual liberty, of social justice versus economic freedom, lies at the bottom of the present tragic division of the world into two hostile camps: "Communist ideology puts the emphasis upon economic justice, and promises that freedom will come automatically after the completion of the revolution. Capitalism puts the emphasis upon freedom, and promises that justice will follow as a by-product of free enterprise; that too is an ideology which has been proved false. It is the responsibility of Christians to seek new, creative solutions which never allow either justice or freedom to destroy the other."[4]

Among the figures which people the pages of Benjamin Franklin's account of his early years in Philadelphia, one of the most shadowy is the benevolent Quaker merchant Thomas Denham, who came to Franklin's rescue in London in 1726 and gave him employment in his store after their return to Philadelphia. Little is known of Denham beyond the few sentences which Franklin devoted to him in his *Autobiography*.[5] Yet the economic philosophy of the man who gave Franklin his first training in business should not pass unnoticed in any account of the man in whom sociologists have seen the classic embodiment of the spirit of modern capitalism.[6] Although we cannot identify the actual economic ideas of Thomas Denham, we can reconstruct the pattern of economic thinking that was characteristic of the eighteenth century mercantile Quakers as a group. In so doing, we shall be describing a complex of ideas that contributed directly to the rise of modern capitalism.

The popular image of the Quaker as a shrewd businessman has a long history. Early in the course of Quakerism, George Fox observed that "Friends had double the trade, beyond any of their neighbours. And if there was any trading, they had it."[7] Opponents of the Quakers delighted in making derogatory comments on their acquisitive talents. The following character of the Quakers, for example, appeared in an enormously popular book first published in England in 1684:

As to these modern Seducers, they are not Men of *Arms* but a herd of silly insignificant People, aiming rather to heap up Riches in Obscurity, than to acquire a Fame by an heroick Undertaking. They are generally Merchants and Mechanicks, and are observed to be very punctual in their Dealings, Men of few Words in a Bargain, modest and compos'd in their Deportment, temperate in their Lives and using great Frugality in all Things. In a Word, they are singularly Industrious, sparing no Labour or Pains to increase their Wealth; and so subtle and inventive, that they would, if possible, extract Gold out of Ashes.[8]

The statement of an English anti-Quaker writer at the end of the seventeenth century that Gracechurch Street Meeting in London was composed of "the *Richest* Trading Men in London," is simply a statement of historical fact. The list of attenders at this meeting, situated in the heart of London's trading and financial district, reads like a beadroll of the most famous banking and commercial families of England; it includes the Barclays, Gurneys, Hanburys, Lloyds, Osgoods, Hoares, Dimsdales, and Christys, to name only the most important.[9]

The reputation for business sagacity followed the Quakers to America. The strongest proof that this reputation was justified can be found in the Philadelphia tax list for 1769. At this period the Quakers constituted no more than one-seventh of Philadelphia's population, but they accounted for more than half of those who paid taxes in excess of £100. Even more striking, perhaps, is the fact that of the seventeen wealthiest individuals in Philadelphia eight were Quakers in good standing and four were men who had been reared as Friends. Only five were non-Quakers, and one of these—William Shippen—owed the basis of his fortune to his Quaker grandfather.

This striking circumstance cannot be explained on the basis of the Quakers' having been "in on the ground floor" by virtue of their early arrival on the Philadelphia scene, for such an explanation is totally inapplicable to the situation of the English Friends, who achieved equal economic success in spite of the persecutions which placed them at a real disadvantage in relation to businessmen of other persuasions. The argument has often been advanced that since Friends were excluded by statute or conscientious scruple from government office and from all the professions except medicine, their best talents were channeled perforce into trade and commerce.[10] Though

not without considerable validity, this argument, in contrast to the
first, applies with peculiar force to the English Quakers, but is subject
to a number of significant exceptions when applied to Friends in
Pennsylvania. In both the mother country and the colonies, of course,
the professional ministry, the Army, and the Navy were closed to
Friends by reason of specific Quaker testimonies. In Penn's commonwealth, however, no oath of allegiance was required for officeholding,
and for three-quarters of a century most of the important posts in
the provincial government were actually occupied by Quaker merchants. True, there was among the Pennsylvania Quakers some re-
sidual prejudice against lawyers and law courts akin to that which
led George Fox to cry out feelingly: "away with those lawyers,
twenty shilling Councellors, thirty shilling Sergeants, ten groat At-
tourneys, that will throw men into Prison for a thing of nought";[11]
nevertheless, there were a number of outstanding Quaker lawyers
in colonial Pennsylvania like John Kinsey and Nicholas Waln. Furthermore, two Quakers—David Lloyd and James Logan—served as
Chief Justices of the provincial Supreme Court. It is well known that
several of the greatest English physicians of the eighteenth century
were Friends, notably Drs. Fothergill, Lettsom, and Dimsdale, while
in Pennsylvania Dr. Thomas Cadwalader, Dr. Lloyd Zachary, and
Drs. Thomas and Phineas Bond all came from Quaker backgrounds.
Thus the theory that Friends turned to business because every avenue
of professional life was closed to them hardly stands scrutiny.

Obviously the fundamental reason for Quaker success in business
must be sought in something common to Friends on both sides of the
Atlantic. Where shall we find it but in the religious ethic of Quakerism
itself? It is a commonplace of recent historical writing that an intimate
relationship existed between certain of the distinctive ideas of Protestantism and the rise of modern capitalism. Discussion of this problem has been carried on primarily with reference to the Calvinist
wing of Protestantism. No one has pursued this line of investigation
with respect to Quakerism.

One may begin with the generalization that Quakerism, arising
in the middle of the seventeenth century, was one of the many variant
expressions of the dominant and all-pervasive Puritanism of the age.
Atypical in many respects, it yet shared with Puritanism a common

substratum of religious and social ideas and mental habits, some of which were not wholly compatible with the peculiar doctrines which differentiated Quakerism from Puritan orthodoxy. Although Friends believed that the substance of their ethical ideas was the product in each instance of immediate revelation, it is undeniable that in many respects the form and framework in which the ideas were expressed were those of Puritanism. In other words, as Richard B. Schlatter puts it, "puritans who turned Quaker did not shed their puritanism."[12]

Like other Puritans, Friends looked upon the material world of daily toil and daily bread as God's world in which men were called to do His will. There are few more vigorous expressions of the Protestant attitude toward monastic rejection of the world than William Penn's attack upon the "religious bedlams" in which monks practiced what he called "a lazy, rusty, unprofitable self-denial, burdensome to others to feed their idleness."

The Christian convent and monastery [he insisted] are within, where the soul is encloistered from sin; and this religious house the true followers of Christ carry about with them, who exempt not themselves from the conversation of the world, though they keep themselves from the evil of the world in their conversation. . . . True godliness don't turn men out of the world, but enables them to live better in it, and excites their endeavors to mend it.[13]

God's will, in other words, could be carried out as faithfully on the wharves and in the warehouses and counting rooms of Philadelphia as anywhere else. Friends were adjured to remember, however, that this world was transitory and that their hearts should not be set upon its evanescent goods but upon eternal treasures. "So every one strive to be rich in the life, and in the kingdom and things of the world that hath no end . . ." wrote George Fox to the merchants in 1661; "And therefore, let him that buys, or sells, or possesses, or uses this world, be as if he did not." This was, of course, no other than the doctrine of loving the world with "weaned affections" which, we are told, was "a staple moral of Puritan discourse."[14]

This *innerweltliche Askese* was an integral part of the way of life which the Quakers brought over to Philadelphia. Israel Pemberton, so-called "King of the Quakers," writing in 1749 about a severe financial loss occasioned by the sinking of one of his ships, summed up this aspect of the economic ethic of the Quaker merchants in classic form. Experiences of this sort, he declared,

tend to wean the Mind from delighting in transitories and if rightly improv'd dispose us to look after Enjoyments more certain and permanent. . . . I am sensible there's a Satisfaction and I believe Something of a duty, in doing for ourselves: The Principle of True Religion being Active and never disposes the Mind to Indolence and Sloth, but it likewise Leads us to Consider, I may say often reminds us of the End and Purpose of our Views and Pursuits, and Reproves us for them, if not Consistent with the one Point to which they ought Solely to tend, the Honour of God and Good of Mankind.[15]

Here are the "weaned affections," the "active principle" of true religion, the "duty" of economic activity, and the end thereof conceived in terms of "the Honour of God." Neither Richard Baxter nor John Cotton could have quarreled with any of the sentiments of this pious Quaker.

The Puritan concept of the "calling" as the task in life to which each individual was summoned by God was taken for granted by the Quakers.

All Friends [wrote George Fox] in the wisdom of God train up your children in the fear of God . . . and as they are capable, they may be instructed and kept employed in some lawful calling, that they may be diligent, serving the Lord in the things that are good; that none may live idle, and be destroyers of the creation. . . .[16]

No lawful occupation was too gross or too menial to have been appointed by God for His service: "the perfection of Christian life," declared William Penn, "extends to every honest labor or traffic used among men."[17] We owe to Thomas Chalkley, Quaker minister, sea captain, and merchant, our most representative Quaker rationale of the calling:

We have Liberty from God, and his dear Son lawfully, and for Accommodation's Sake, to work or seek for food or Raiment; tho' that ought to be a Work of Indifferency, compar'd to the great Work of Salvation. Our Saviour saith, *Labour not for the Meat which perisheth, but for that which endureth for ever, or to eternal Life:* By which we do not understand, that Christians must neglect their necessary Occasions and their outward Trades and Callings; but that their chief Labour, and greatest Concern ought to be for their future Well-being in his glorious Kingdom; else why did our Lord say to his Disciples, *Children, have you any Meat?* They answered, *No;* and he bid them *cast their Nets into the Sea, and they drew to Land a Net full of great Fishes;* and Fishing being their Trade, no doubt they sold them, for it was not likely they could eat 'em all themselves. . . . By this, and much more, which might be noted, it appears that we not only have Liberty to labour in Moderation, but we are given to understand, that it is our Duty so to do. The Farmer, the Tradesman, and the Merchant, do not understand by our Lord's Doctrine, that they must neglect their Calling, or grow idle in their Business, but must certainly work, and be industrious in their Callings.[18]

If one kept one's inner eye single to the Lord, and labored diligently in one's calling, one could expect that God would show His favor by adding His blessing in the form of material prosperity. And, conversely, business success could be regarded as a visible sign that one was indeed living "in the Light." Chalkley's *Journal* contains many entries like the following: "After these several Journeys were over . . . I was some Time at Home, and followed my Business with Diligence and Industry, and throve in the Things of the World, the Lord adding a Blessing to my Labour."[19] Thus by God's blessing the faithful and diligent Friend, living plainly in accordance with "the simplicity of Truth," almost inevitably accumulated wealth "for the Honour of God and Good of Mankind." James Logan, Penn's erstwhile secretary and a great dealer in furs and skins, confided to an English correspondent that he looked upon it as a particular Providence in his favor that he had been led into the Indian trade; "should I with open eyes," he added, "give away those advantages that by God's Blessing my own Industry and management have . . . thrown on me to others who have had no part in that Management . . . I could never account for it to my Self and family."[20]

The virtues of industry and frugality were, of course, held in high repute among Friends. Idleness was looked upon with horror as the breeder of vice and a vain conversation; diligence in a warrantable calling was considered a religious duty. Thomas Chalkley, our seagoing Quaker, quoted earlier, linked the religious closely with the secular life and associated the virtue of diligence with both: "I followed my Calling; and kept to Meetings diligently; for I was not

easy to be idle; either in my spiritual or temporal Callings."²¹ Frugality
was usually recommended on religious grounds as being essential to
that austere simplicity of life which "Truth" demanded. Occasionally,
however, it was justified on more practical grounds, as tending to
increase one's capital and credit. Isaac Norris, a great Quaker merchant in early colonial Philadelphia, revealed something of this mo-
tivation when he advised his son, just starting out on his first business
trip to London: "thou must remember that the more frugall thou art
the more will be thy Stock. . . . Come back plain. This will be a
reputation to thee and recommend thee to the best and most Sensible
people."²² One remembers Benjamin Franklin's explanation of the
methods by which he had established his reputation just after leaving
Thomas Denham's employ: "In order to secure my credit and character as a tradesman," he wrote, "I took care not only to be in *reality*
industrious and frugal, but to avoid all appearances to the contrary.
I drest plainly. . . ."²³

Prudence, honesty, and a strong sense of order, were the other
virtues which contributed to Quaker business success. Friends were
known for extreme caution in their business undertakings. Their book
of discipline contained a standing advice against buying, bargaining,
or contracting beyond one's abilities, and in their meetings for discipline Friends were constantly warned against imprudent ventures by
the query: "Are Friends careful to live within the Bounds of their
Circumstances, and to avoid launching into Trade or Business beyond
their ability to manage?"²⁴ If a Friend were so imprudent as to find
himself forced into bankruptcy, he stood in danger of disownment by
the meeting. Thus prudence had its spiritual as well as its temporal
sanctions.

Because Quaker businessmen were known to be scrupulously honest, people were glad to deal with them. From almost the very beginning, as George Fox records, "people came to see Friends' honesty
and truthfulness . . . they knew and saw that, for conscience sake
towards God, they would not cozen and cheat them."²⁵ Paradoxically,
it was probably this very virtue of strict truthfulness that gave
Friends the reputation for slyness and dishonesty. Because they
cherished such a respect for the truth in its stark simplicity, Quakers
were characteristically men of few words: "they recommended
silence by their example," wrote William Penn, "having very few

words upon all occasions."[26] It is not difficult to understand how the uncommunicative Quaker could come to seem secretive and subtle, and consequently how the suspicion of slyness and dishonesty could be built into the legend of the Quaker businessman. It is especially easy after reading the advice of John Reynell, Philadelphia Quaker merchant, to his apprentice:

In doing business be a little on the Reserve, and Observe well the Person thou has to do with. . . . Keep thy Business to thy self, and don't let it be known, who thou dost Business for, or what Sorts of Goods thou Ships off. Some will want to know both, perhaps with a Design to Circumvent thee. Endeavour to know what Prices other People give for Goods, but say nothing of what thou givest thy self, or where thou buys. . . . If thou finds out a Place where they Sell cheap, keep it to thy Self, for if thou Ships off Goods cheaper than others, it will increase Business.[27]

A sympathetic French visitor to Philadelphia shortly after the American Revolution called attention to "the order which the Quakers are accustomed from childhood to apply to the distribution of their tasks, their thoughts, and every moment of their lives. They carry this spirit of order everywhere," he continued; "it economizes time, activity and money."[28] This virtue was essential for success in a modern "rationalized" capitalist economy in which the pursuit of gain was a more or less continuous intensive activity, based upon the expectation of regular production, markets, and profits. Again one cannot help recalling Benjamin Franklin, who gave "order" third place in his catalogue of virtues, adding this appropriate precept: "Let all your things have their places; let each part of your business have its time."[29]

*   *   *

Some years after the Revolution, the unfinished manuscript of Franklin's autobiography happened to fall into the hands of Abel James, a Philadelphia Quaker merchant and son-in-law of our maritime Friend Thomas Chalkley. He recognized at once how consummately it inculcated virtues which Friends held in high regard, and urged Franklin to complete and publish it, adding "the influence writings under that class have on the minds of youth is very great, and has nowhere appeared to me so plain as in our public friends [that is, Quaker ministers'] journals." He concluded with a eulogy of Franklin which showed how thoroughly he was in sympathy with the formula for business success worked out by the erstwhile protégé of Friend Thomas Denham: "I know of no character living," wrote the good Quaker, ". . . who has so much in his power as thyself to promote a greater spirit of industry and early attention to business, frugality, and temperance with the American youth."[30]

II. QUAKERISM AND THE "NEW PHILOSOPHY"

When George Fox described in his *Journal* the moment of vision in which it was inwardly made known to him that there was One, even Christ Jesus, who could "speak to his condition," he concluded his account of the revelation with the words: "And this I knew *experimentally*." At almost precisely the same time, a group of scientifically minded men was beginning to hold regular meetings at Gresham College in London to discuss "Physick, Anatomy, Geometry, Astronomy, Navigation, Staticks, Magnetics, Chymicks, Mechanicks, and Natural Experiments." This group of men, devotees of the "New Philosophy" of experimental science, was the nucleus of the Royal Society, incorporated a few years later and destined to become the world's foremost scientific organization. Probably Fox knew little of their work, then or later, though he may have made an oblique reference to it in 1672 when he wrote of "the Royal Society indeed," by which he meant a divine-human society which would be "above all Societies that Nations, Peoples, Tongues and Languages have made, in which there is Discord."[31] Yet the Quaker appeal from religious authority and tradition to direct experience is clearly akin to the method of experimentation by which the Greshamites shook off the shackles of scholastic tradition and authority and made possible the advances of modern science.

The kinship of Quakerism and science over the past three centuries can easily be documented. Between 1663 and 1915 no less than fifty-eight Friends were granted the coveted Fellowship of the Royal Society—a far larger number in proportion to the size of the denomination than any other religious group could show.[32] Among them were such distinguished scientists as John Dalton, the first formulator of modern atomic theory in chemistry; Joseph Lister, the founder of modern antiseptic surgery; and Sir Arthur Stanley Eddington, the astrophysicist. On this side of the Atlantic one thinks of John Bartram, who scoured the American colonies in search of new plants; of Edward Drinker Cope, who helped to lay the groundwork for modern paleontology; of William James Beal, whose fundamental research in plant genetics provided the scientific basis for the marvels of modern hybridization.

Quaker educational theory and practice have always given a prominent place to natural science. When George Fox himself founded the first Quaker schools in England, he included it as a basic part of the curriculum; and two centuries later, when a group of American Friends founded Swarthmore College, the seal they adopted for the institution reflected, perhaps inadvertently, the importance they attached to science, for it displays a microscope, a telescope, and a chemical retort, these symbols almost crowding out the scrolls which stand for the other traditional liberal arts. At a time when American educators, alarmed by Russia's apparent lead in the production of scientists, are zealously—perhaps too zealously—giving thought to the role of science in American education, it is worth remembering that this emphasis has always been present in Quaker education.

But it is also worth remembering that the zeal of the Friends for scientific knowledge, promoted, as the following discussion shows, by their experimental attitude toward truth and by the dictates of the "Protestant ethic," has seldom been divorced from their concern for the humane and the spiritual. John Bartram's motive for seeking out new plants, apart from simple curiosity, was the hope of adding new curative and pain-relieving drugs to the pharmacopoeia. Warder Clyde Allee, a distinguished Quaker biologist at the University of Chicago, could not publish his findings concerning the role of co-operation among animals without discussing their bearing on the problems of the human community, especially on international relations and the possibility of eliminating war. Sir Arthur Eddington's best-known book is called *Science and the Unseen World*.

Soon after the work of the nuclear physicist was first put to dire use over Hiroshima and Nagasaki, it became apparent to many that American science was becoming inextricably linked with preparations for cataclysmic war. A large number of Quaker scientists, "feeling a compelling need for drawing some line between destructive and constructive work in their own professional lives," joined with other like-minded scientific workers to form the Society for Social Responsibility in Science, an organization whose basic "concern" is clear from its name.[33] If our culture is coming increasingly to be dominated by science, it may well be that Quakerism, having contributed to its growth, also has something to contribute to its humanization.

The rise of experimental science in England was roughly contemporaneous with the ascendency of Puritanism, of which Quakerism was one variant expression. This fact was once regarded merely as an interesting coincidence without much significance. More recently it has come to be recognized that there was a positive connection between religion and the rise of the "new philosophy" of experimental science. The argument in this essay is that there was a particularly close correlation between the religious ethos of Quakerism and the demonstrable aptitude of Friends for scientific pursuits. As in my discussion of Quakerism and economic life, the contention is not that scientific activity was directly the product of Quakerism in the sense of being the second term in a cause-and-effect relationship, but rather, to quote a contemporary sociologist, "that the religious ethic, considered as a social force, so consecrated science as to make it a highly respected and laudable focus of attention."[34] The most significant area of agreement between the Quaker-Puritan position and that of modern science as it emerged at the end of the seventeenth century lay, I shall attempt to show, in the combination of the empirical temper with the method of rationalism.

Some of the generalizations which appear in my discussion of Quakerism and capitalism apply with equal force here. Practical, methodical activity in the world was considered an evidence that one was living "in the Light." The expenditure of physical energy and the handling of material objects was identified with industry,

NOTE: Pages 67–72 of this chapter originally appeared in Chapter 9 of the author's *Meeting House and Counting House: The Quaker Merchants of Colonial Philadelphia* (Chapel Hill: University of North Carolina Press, 1948), pages 205–213. Used by permission.

whereas abstract speculation and contemplation, when not directed toward purely religious ends, was equated with idleness. This distinction coincided in a remarkable way with that between the new experimental science and the older deductive scholastic science. If experimentation was "the scientific expression of the practical, active and methodical bents" of the Puritan,[35] it was equally so of the Quaker. In this aspect of the Puritan-Quaker ethos the new science found one of its major sanctions.

The connection can be observed most clearly in education. Quaker schools established in the last third of the seventeenth century in England and the colonies were organized around a new educational theory introduced by the Puritans to replace the traditional classical curriculum. The new realistic concept, embodied in the curricula of the dissenting academies, emphasized the empirical and the utilitarian at the expense of the dialectical and the humanistic.[36] *Things* rather than words were the stuff of education, and Baconian science, with its experimental, antischolastic basis, naturally found a place in the reformed curriculum. There is no positive evidence that Quaker leaders or schoolmasters were influenced by the treatises of John Durie, Sir William Petty, Samuel Hartlib, and the other reformers, but there is abundant evidence that the Quaker theory of education was in harmony with their insistence upon "the importance of dealing sensibly with concrete and material things, of actually expending energy in the pursuit of truth . . . in contrast to the non-physical activity . . . of those who sought truth in books and the mind."[37]

William Penn was a friend of both Durie and Petty, and the similarity of his ideas to theirs is too obvious to be overlooked. Like them, he had no patience with "the vain Quiddities, idle and gross Terms, and most sophistical Ways of Syllogizing, with the rest of that useless and injurious Pedantry (to Mankind, brought into the Christian Religion by Popish School-men, and so eminently in Vogue in *Oxford* and *Cambridge* . . .)."[38] And like them he would emphasize *realia*:

The first thing obvious to children is what is sensible, and that we make no part of their rudiments.

We press their memory too soon, and puzzle, strain, and load them with words and rules, to know grammar and rhetoric and a strange tongue or two, that it is ten to one may never be useful to them, leaving their natural genius to mechanical and physical or natural knowledge uncultivated and neglected, which would be of exceeding use and pleasure to them through the whole course of their life.

To be sure, languages are not to be despised or neglected, but things are still to be preferred.[39]

Insistence on the priority of things over words was such a cardinal principle in Quaker thinking that Emerson could later describe George Fox succinctly and accurately as "a realist putting ever a thing for a form."[40] William Penn described Fox as "a divine and a naturalist," and added that although he was "ignorant of useless and sophistical science," he had in him "the grounds of useful and commendable knowledge." He had often been surprised, he confessed, at Fox's "questions and answers in natural things."[41] That Fox's philosophy of education included the utilitarian and scientific emphases is clear from his proposals for the first Quaker schools at Waltham Abbey and Shacklewell, where the object, in his words, was to provide instruction "in whatsoever things were civil and useful in the creation."[42]

The scientific impulse was closely allied with a humanitarian concern for the development of medicine. This motive is clearly apparent in Fox's proposal for a school which would teach, besides languages, "the nature of herbs, roots, plants, and trees."[43] This projected school was probably the one to which the Quaker botanist Thomas Lawson referred in 1690:

Now some years ago, George ffox, William Pen, and others, were concerned to purchase a piece of land near London for the use of a Garden Schoolhouse and a dwelling-house for the Master, in which garden, one or two or more of every sorte of our English plants were to be planted, as also many outlandish plants. My purpose was to write a book on these in Latin, so as a boy had the description of these in book-lessons, and their vertues, he might see these growing in the garden, or plantation, to gain the knowledge of them: but persecutions and troubles obstructed the prosecution hereof, which the Master of Christ's College in Cambridge hearing of, told me was a noble and honorable undertaking, and would fill the Nation with Philosophers.[44]

If the theory of education underlying this scheme has a contemporary ring, it is because its assumptions are essentially the same as those of modern progressive education.

The arguments by which Puritans and Quakers vindicated the place of science in education were also used to recommend scientific study and experimentation as a form of recreation.[45] The high standard of personal morality which the Quakers set for themselves kept them away from the playhouse, the ballroom, the gambling den, and the bull pit. Scientific study as an avocation had the virtues of being useful, of exercising the mental powers, and, by revealing God's plan in the natural world, of promoting a reverent frame of mind. Hence Robert Barclay could recommend as "innocent Divertisements, which may sufficiently serve for Relaxation of the Mind . . . To follow after Gardening, To use Geometrical and Mathematical Experiments, and such other things of this Nature."[46] And William Penn allowed that to "study moderately such commendable and profitable arts as navigation, arithmetic, geometry, husbandry, gardening, handicraft, medicine, etc." was a form of recreation consistent with Truth.[47]

If the empirical bent of the Quakers tended to render the method of the "new philosophy" congenial to them, a certain rational character inherent in the mental habits of at least some of them provided a frame of mind conducive to its prosecution. To speak of rationalism in connection with a religious group usually regarded as the most mystical of Protestant sects may seem paradoxical. It can be granted that there was little of the rational about George Fox and the first generation of Friends. For them man's rational faculty was of little use. It could never light the way to Truth: that was the function of the Spirit alone. But with Robert Barclay and William Penn of the second generation we come into a different intellectual atmosphere. Reason for them had its uses. Though it could not by itself lead men to the Truth, absolute and eternal, it could at least guide them to an understanding of truths, relative truths about the temporal world; and it could confirm and vindicate what the Light revealed.

For Barclay man's natural reason was a sort of secondary light, subordinate to the Divine Light and incapable by itself of leading to a saving knowledge of God. Nevertheless, he hastened to add, "we do not hereby affirm, as if Man had received his Reason to no purpose, or to be of no service unto him, in no wise: We look upon Reason as fit to order and rule Man in things Natural."[48] In the realm of nature, therefore—the realm with which science concerned itself—reason was a trustworthy instrument, and man was free to use it.

In William Penn's writings reason was given even broader scope. Ordinarily Penn maintained a clear distinction between the Inner Light and natural reason, but occasionally the lines blurred. In *The Sandy Foundation Shaken* and *The Christian Quaker* Penn appealed frankly to right reason to establish his doctrine of the Inner Light, and in another controversial work he declared flatly that "God is the Fountain as well of Reason as Light. And we assert our Principle not to be without Reason, but most Reasonable."[49] What could be more typical of the spirit of free rational inquiry associated with the "new philosophy" than these words from *More Fruits of Solitude:* "Truth never lost ground by inquiry because she is most of all reasonable"?[50]

Since man is endowed by God with natural reason in addition to the Inner Light, these Friends argued, it behooves him to utilize it to God's glory and his own benefit. "It were happy," wrote Penn, "if we studied nature more in natural things, and acted according to nature, whose rules are few, plain, and most reasonable." By thus applying reason to the study of nature, man would the better understand "the heavens, earth, and waters with their respective, various, and numerous inhabitants, their productions, natures, seasons, sympathies, and antipathies, their use, benefit, and pleasure." Moreover (and in this conviction the religious ethos provided the most potent sanction for the furtherance of natural science), "an eternal wisdom, power, majesty, and goodness [become] very conspicuous to us through these sensible and passing forms, the world wearing the mark of its Maker, Whose stamp is everywhere visible and the characters very legible to the children of wisdom."[51]

Although seldom articulated as such, the doctrine of Providence as the undergirding and sustaining presence of God in nature was one of the premises of Quaker as of all Puritan thought, providing a basis for what in other religious traditions was to be called "natural theology."[52] If, as A. N. Whitehead has said, a living science requires "a widespread instinctive conviction in the existence of an *Order of Things*, and in particular, of an *Order of Nature*,"[53] one can see how some of the basic assumptions of Quakerism promoted a habit of thinking congenial to the reception of the new science.

In view of the community of assumptions and the parallelism of method in the Quaker ethos and the "new philosophy," it is hardly surprising to discover that on November 2, 1682, less than a year before he set sail for Pennsylvania, William Penn was "propounded Candidate" for the Royal Society and elected a member of that chief nursery of the new science.[54] Penn's activity in connection with the Royal Society appears to have been slight, although he is known to have been personally acquainted with a number of the more prominent Fellows, including Sir William Petty, Robert Hooke, Robert Wood, Edward Bernard, John Aubrey, Dr. John Wallis, Sir Isaac Newton, and John Locke. Still, if any further evidence is needed of the scientific temper of Penn's mind, it is abundantly provided in a letter which he wrote to John Aubrey from Philadelphia, a few months after his arrival there in 1682:

I value my selfe much upon the good opinion of those Ingeneous Gentlemen I know of the Royall Society, and their kind wishes for me and my poor Provinces: all I can say is that I and it are votarys to the prosperity of their harmless and usefull inquierys. It is even one step to Heaven to returne to Nature and Though I love that proportion should be observed in all things, yett a naturall Knowledge, or the Science of things from sence and a carefull observation and argumentation thereon, reinstates men, and gives them some possession of themselves againe: a thing they have long wanted by an ill Tradition, too closely followed and the foolish Credulity so Incident to men.

Penn then put his finger upon the basic identity between the method of the new science and the appeal to immediate experience which was the core of Quakerism. Making a frank avowal of his loyalty to the experimental method in both the natural and the supernatural spheres, he wrote: "I am a Greshamist throughout; I Love Inquiry, not for inquiry's sake, but care not to trust my share in either world to other men's Judgments, at Least without having a finger in the Pye for myself."[55]

CHAPTER V

The Quaker Esthetic

The Quaker, having found God in the simplicity of the Inward Light, worshiped Him in the simplicity of silent waiting and adoration: no anthems, no hymns, no organ music; no elaborately carved pulpit or stained-glass windows or religious images. The typical Quaker meetinghouse was a plain structure furnished with rows of plain benches on which a plainly dressed people waited in silence until someone should be moved to speak in plain words what the Divine Spirit vouchsafed to him (or her) for the edification of the worshiping group. The simplicity of their worship carried over into the daily existence of the Friends to govern their dress, their speech, the furnishing of their houses, their whole way of life.

No doubt their lives were impoverished by their deliberate rejection of their cultural heritage in music, literature, and the fine arts. In its time the early Quaker witness for simplicity was a valid protest against the tendency of men and women in other religious traditions to substitute sensuous enjoyment for spiritual perception, to let their minds and spirits be distracted from religious truth by the pleasures of the ear, the eye, and the imagination. Later, however, the testimony for plainness hardened into a dogma, and what had been a protest against forms became itself a rigid form.

It was not until the end of the nineteenth century that pianos were allowed in Quaker schools, and it is only within the past two decades that music and the fine arts have been admitted to the curricula of the Eastern Quaker colleges as full-fledged, legitimate disciplines. Friends are beginning, however, to realize what they have been missing by excluding a whole segment of experience from their lives. In recent years, for example, the *a cappella* choir of Earlham College has performed during Philadelphia Yearly Meeting (not, of course, as part

73

of a meeting for worship), and a Quaker Fellowship of the Arts has exhibited paintings and sculptures at the sessions of London Yearly Meeting.

Yet there is still a place in our modern culture—in the arts and in everyday life—for a religious testimony for simplicity. Much of modern architecture, after all, is only a reassertion of the principle which guided the builders of the early Quaker meetinghouses. And as our affluent society threatens to engulf us in a multiplicity of material things that we don't need and our public-relations industry to drown us in a flood of debased words, there is renewed relevance to the query with which Friends regularly examine their fidelity to this testimony: "Do you keep to simplicity and moderation in your speech, your manner of living, and your pursuit of business?"

1

There is perhaps something pretentious or paradoxical in speaking of a Quaker esthetic. The Quaker genius has obviously expressed itself in realms other than the artistic, and the immense corpus of Quaker writing is characteristically concerned with the good and the true, almost to the exclusion of the beautiful. Indeed there is a sense in which the thrust of early Quakerism was distinctly antiesthetic— indifferent, if not downright hostile, to sensuous beauty—just as there is a sense in which it was basically anti-intellectual—distrustful of reason, and consequently uninterested in working out a rationale of the beautiful.

One can best understand the attitude of the Friends if one starts by locating Quakerism in the spectrum of Protestant thought. In its origin it was an integral part of the movement we call Puritanism, the left wing, the radical extreme, of that pervasive phenomenon in the religious life of seventeenth century England and America. The Quaker took his stand on the essential affirmation of the Puritan—that God through the Holy Spirit could regenerate man, could give him an immediate knowledge of His Truth. The Quaker called this direct experience of divine grace the Inward Light. He differed from the more conservative Puritan chiefly, but crucially, in maintaining that this Light was accessible to all men, and not merely to a few elected saints. Having made his central affirmation, he could dispense with the sophisticated and fine-spun theological apparatus of Calvinism, the involutions and intellectual subleties that make New England Puritan thought so stimulating a study in the hands of modern interpreters like Perry Miller. He had little interest in "reasoning high/Of Providence, Foreknowledge, Will, and Fate,/Fixed fate, free will, fore-knowledge absolute." For him this sort of intellectual game was "Vain wisdom all, and false philosophy." It was enough for the Quaker that he heard God's voice in his own breast, that he had a means of apprehending divine Truth intuitively. He had no need to invoke human reason or Scriptural authority to establish his faith or to work out its implications: his religion was, quite simply, a matter of experience, of direct illumination. It is in this sense that Quakerism can be called anti-intellectual (even though, as we have seen, some early Friends allowed man's reason a subordinate place in tracing the design of God's natural universe).

If the early Quakers went far beyond the other English Protestants in bypassing the intellect in religious matters, they out-Puritaned the Puritans in their attitude toward what they called the "world"—and what we mean perhaps by that comprehensive term "culture." They were ultra-Protestant in their conviction that, though one must live in the midst of the world, one must never let its attractions clog the channels of the Spirit. For the Quakers, as for all Puritans, life was a pilgrimage, and, no matter how enticing or delightsome the beauties of this world might be, the pilgrim must never let his attention be distracted from the beauty of holiness, the end and purpose of his journey. "The true followers of Christ," wrote William Penn, ". . . exempt not themselves from the conversation of the world, though they keep themselves from the evil of the world in their conversation. . . . " This was the burden of his great moral tract *No Cross, No Crown:* "The Cross of Christ . . . truly overcomes the world and leads a life of purity in the face of its allurements."[1]

It followed for the Quaker, as for any Puritan, that he should love the world with "weaned affections"; he must be careful not to let his sensibilities linger in sensuous appreciation upon the fading things of this world, lest he forget the lasting beauty that existed only in the world of the spirit. All Puritans distrusted the unfettered imagination; to Richard Sibbes it was "a wild and ranging thing," to Thomas Hooker, "the forge of villainy . . . the warehouse of wickedness . . . the Sea of all abominations, which overflows into all the Sences."[2] And Robert Barclay, the Quaker theologian, agreed that all the imaginations of the natural man were "evil perpetually in the sight of God."[3] If the typical Puritan disciplined his imagination, if he curbed his esthetic sensibilities, lest he become too much in love with the world, the Quaker went still further in austerity. If the Presbyterian or Congregationalist banished all religious imagery from his churches, all music (except the psalms of David) from his services, all verbal embroidery from his sermons, the Quaker stripped his worship life down to the stark simplicity of silent communion with God in a bare meetinghouse. It is in this sense that Quakerism can be called antiesthetic. If we deplore—as most modern Quakers do—the impoverishment of life, the starving of the senses that resulted from this ultra-Puritanical suspicion of sensuous experience, we do well to remember that the early Quaker had another kind of experience, a supernal vision of the "simplicity of Truth" which completely satisfied his soul's longing for beauty. And in the light of the revolutions in taste which have occurred since the eighteenth century, we can recognize that actually the Quaker ideas were not antiesthetic at all, but reflected an ideal of functional simplicity peculiarly congenial to modern sensibilities.

2

To find the roots of the Quaker esthetic we must start with the central religious idea of the Friends—the idea, or rather the experience, of the Inner Light, that glint of the divine effulgence shining in the souls of men, giving them knowledge of God's will for their guidance, leading them, as they believed, into purity of life, and, as it were, restoring among them the conditions that had prevailed among the primitive Christians. Because the early Quaker conceived of religion in terms of spiritual experience and the difference it made in a man's daily life, rather than in terms of intellectual "notions" about the things of God, there were no distinctive Quaker doctrines, apart from the central one of the indwelling Light. But there were

distinctive ways of behaving, which the Quaker called "testimonies."
I need only mention the rejection of all war and violence, the principled refusal to swear judicial oaths, to pay tithes, to use flattering
terms of address and conventional gestures of respect, the consistent
use of *thou* and *thee* to all men, regardless of social station. Howard
Brinton, a modern Quaker writer, has usefully arranged these distinctive Quaker testimonies under the headings of Equality, Harmony
or Peace, Community, and Simplicity.[4]

It is with simplicity as a religious testimony that we are concerned. The first Friends had no hesitation about referring to their
religious message categorically as *Truth*. Their early preachers, the
reader will recall, were called "Publishers of Truth"; and when
George Fox was successful in converting large numbers of people,
he took no credit to himself but said simply, "The Truth was over all."
One of the principal attributes of Truth was simplicity. The phrase
"the simplicity of Truth" crops up again and again in early Quaker
writing. "Simplicity," says Howard Brinton, "meant the absence of
all that was unnecessary, such as ornamentation in dress, speech, manners, architecture, house furnishings."[5] The ideal of simplicity was
closely related to the Quaker concern for social justice. "The very
trimming of the vain world," wrote William Penn, "would clothe all
the naked one."[6] And so the early Friends dressed plainly—not in the
standardized "plain dress" of a later period, the broad-brimmed hat
and lapel-less "shadbelly" coat, the coal-scuttle bonnet and cap, the
plain shawl and dove-gray gown, that ultimately became a kind of
Quaker uniform, but in the ordinary costume of the day stripped of
all superfluities and useless ornaments. Their very speech and style
of writing they conscientiously reduced to this standard of simplicity.
"Ye that dwell in the light and walk in the light," George Fox exhorted
his followers, "use plainness of speech and plain words."[7]

Now of course this insistence on plainness, though carried to an
extreme by the Friends, was by no means exclusively a Quaker trait.
It was part of a strong current of taste in the seventeenth century, a
current that ran counter to the exuberance of the baroque, about
which the art historians have understandably preoccupied themselves.
The "plain style," whether in architecture or prose or the minor arts,
was a Protestant style. The baroque was associated with the Counter-
reformation, and good Protestants rejected it as a work of the Devil,

along with the Mass, the worship of images, and every other manifestation of popery. Professor Garvan, who has rescued the Protestant plain style in church building from its undeserved obscurity, has shown us how it flourished in all its austere strength and purity in seventeenth century Holland and England and how it was carried to New England by the Puritans.[8] I will only observe here that the Quaker meetinghouse in its utter functional simplicity represents the ultimate development of that style, in which, to quote Professor Garvan, "space was closely defined, linear and well-lighted; ornamentation was constrained and abstract; and construction direct, simple, and apparent."[9]

Students of English literature have long been aware of the reform of prose style which occurred toward the end of the seventeenth century. It was a conscious rejection of the euphuistic manner of the Elizabethan Age with its far-fetched tropes, its curious inkhorn terms, its learned quotations, and other rhetorical trappings. More immediately, it was a movement away from the rich verbal textures which Anglican divines like John Donne and Lancelot Andrewes had woven in their sermons. It was a deliberate effort to achieve simplicity and economy, an uncluttered and workmanlike manner of discourse. Many influences converged to effect these revolutionary changes in diction and style, but chief among them were Puritanism in religion and the "new philosophy" of experimental science, and we have come to realize how closely these two forces were intertwined. William Penn, who was both an ultra-Puritan in his religion and a Fellow of the Royal Society, reflected both of these influences when he cautioned writers to avoid artificial eloquence and rhetorical excess and keep to the "simplicity of Truth" in language:

> There is a truth and beauty in rhetoric, but it oftener serves ill turns than good ones.
> Elegancy is a good mien and address given to matters, be it by proper or figurative speech; where the words are apt and allusions very natural, certainly it has a moving grace, but it is too artificial for simplicity, and oftentimes for truth. . . .
> 'Tis certain truth is least indebted to it, because she has least need of it and least uses it.
> But it is a reprovable delicacy in them that despise truth in plain clothes.[10]

The Quaker theory of literary expression was clearly a part of the pervasive counter-baroque movement in the esthetic of the seventeenth century, and it was rooted in the Quaker religious vision of Truth in its austere simplicity.

Of Quaker theory as applied to the other fine arts—to painting, sculpture, music, poetry, and the drama—there is almost nothing to be said, for the early Friends banished them almost totally from their lives. For the arts of architecture and prose writing there was at least the defense of utility; but for the arts whose chief purpose was to please the senses they had nothing but scorn, mingled, one suspects, with a touch of fear—fear of becoming entangled with the winsome delights of the "world" if they once gave way to the human appetite for sensuous beauty.

There are no Quaker painters until Edward Hicks, the nineteenth century "primitive" artist of "The Peaceable Kingdom," and his journal and letters are full of agonizings of spirit over what he considered his unfortunate weakness for creative expression with brush and canvas. "If the Christian world was in the real spirit of Christ," he could write, quite in the spirit of the early Friends, "I do not believe there would be such a thing as a fine painter in christendom. It appears clearly to me to be one of those trifling, insignificant arts, which has never been of any substantial advantage to mankind."[11] Benjamin West, who was born of Quaker parents, is no exception to this generalization: his painting was clearly part of his deliberate rejection of his Quaker upbringing. There are no Quaker sculptors until Patience Wright, the wax-modeler, and she, like Benjamin West, had to flee from her Quaker environment to the court of George III to find an atmosphere in which she could work. And Abigail Adams's characterization of her as the "Queen of Sluts" does not suggest the pious Quakeress! One will look in vain, until very recent times, for Quaker composers or musicians. Ever since George Fox was "moved to cry against all kinds of music, for it burdeneth the pure life," most Quakers have been tone deaf on principle. "Music," wrote Thomas Clarkson at the opening of the nineteenth century, ". . . does not appear to [Friends] to be productive of elevated thoughts, that is, of such thoughts as raise the mind to sublime and spiritual things, abstracted from the inclinations, the temper, and the prejudices of the world. . . . All true elevation . . . can only come, in the opinion of

the Quakers, from the divine source."[12] As for imaginative literature—
novels, lyric poetry, the drama—it is enough to cite the rhetorical
question with which William Penn put an end to discussion on this
matter for good Quakers: "How many plays did Jesus Christ and his
apostles recreate themselves at? What poets [*sic*], romances, com-
edies, and the like did the apostles and saints make or use to pass
away their time withal?"[13]

3

I turn now to what are called—I hope without condescension—
the minor arts. If a Quaker painter, composer, or dramatist is almost
a contradiction in terms, at least in the early years of the movement,
there were a great many Quaker craftsmen—cabinetmakers, joiners, silversmiths, clockmakers, and the like. In fact, the majority of
the early Friends who were not farmers came from the artisan class.
There was no religious testimony to discourage the pursuit of these
callings; indeed, their very utilitarian character made them appear
lawful, if not preferred, callings in the sight of the Lord. And the
ideal of strict integrity which the Inward Light held before the early
Quakers tended to make them excellent workmen, whom the "world's
people" were glad to patronize even though they were dangerous
heretics.[14]

Their religious faith, to be sure, imposed some limitations upon
the Quaker craftsmen. Humphrey Bache, a London goldsmith, for
example, refused to make rings and toys for those whom he considered "proud and vain people."[15] The tailor's calling was a particularly sensitive one because it was so subject to the tyranny of fashion.
Gilbert Latey, a London court tailor, after his "convincement" as a
Friend, declined to make clothes for men of the world who wanted
"their apparel set off with much cost and superfluities of lace and
ribbons."[16] In 1672, a dozen Quaker tailors of London, after holding
a meeting "to discourse of trades and callings," issued a joint epistle
urging all Quakers in the needle trades to free themselves "from
those burthens that many yet groan under, as lace, ribbons, and needless buttons, altogether useless; and such like things which the Light
doth not justify."[17] With one voice the leaders of the Society all exhorted Friends to avoid the vain fashions of the world. "Mind that

which is sober and modest," said George Fox, "and keep to your plain fashions. . . . Take heed of the world's fashions, lest ye be moulded up into their spirit, and that will bring you to slight Truth."[18] Robert Barclay declared categorically that "superfluous" things like ribbons and lace were "altogether unlawful and unsuitable to Christians."[19] And William Penn appealed once more to the example of the "holy men and women" of the Bible:

How many pieces of ribbon, feathers, lace bands, and the like [he asked] had Adam and Eve in Paradise or out of it? What rich embroideries, silks, points, etc., had Abel, Enoch, Noah, and good old Abraham? Did Eve, Sarah, Susanna, Elizabeth, and the Virgin Mary use to curl, powder, patch, paint, wear false locks of strange colors, rich points, trimmings, laced gowns, embroidered petticoats, shoes and slip-slaps laced with silk or silver lace and ruffled like pigeons' feet, with several yards if not pieces of ribbons?[20]

There is little evidence to show the impact of this esthetic of plainness with its strong moral and religious overtones on the cabinet-maker's craft in seventeenth century England or on the kind of furniture the Quakers preferred. But there is some revealing evidence from Ireland, where the insistence on simplicity was carried to the extreme. There, as in England and later in the American colonies, some of the Friends were extraordinarily successful in business, and became wealthy. Material success, wrote William Edmundson, the patriarch of Irish Quakerism, brought into the Society of Friends a spirit that "began to look back into the World . . . and then [appeared] great, fair buildings in City and Country, fine and fashionable Furniture and apparel Equivalent with dainty and voluptuous Provision."[21] The elders of the meetings became alarmed, and took strong measures to check this creeping worldliness. They issued a paper of advice to the household of the faith that was remarkably specific:

As to chests of drawers, they ought to be plain and of one color, without swelling works.

As to tables and chairs, they ought to be all made plain, without carving, keeping out of all new fashions as they come up, and to keep to the fashion that is serviceable.

And as to making great mouldings one above another about press-beds and clock-cases, etc., [they] ought to be avoided, only what is decent according to Truth.

So that all furniture and wainscoting should be all plain and of one color.[22]

They were not content simply to give advice. They appointed committees to "inspect and visit" every Quaker family in the land and labor with them until they should comply with the meeting's requirements. One of these Friends, Joseph Pike, has left an account of how he and his cousin began with their own houses:

Our fine veneeres and garnished cases of drawers, tables, stands, cabinets, scrutoires, &c., we put away, or exchanged for decent plain ones of solid wood without superfluous garnishing or ornamental work; our wainscots or wood-work we had painted of one plain colour, our large mouldings or finishings of panelling, &c.; our swelling chimney-pieces, curiously twisted banisters, we took down, and replaced with useful plain wood-work &c.; our curtains, with valances, drapery, and fringes that we thought too fine, we put away or cut off; our large looking-glasses with decorated frames we sold, or made them into smaller ones; and our closets that were laid out with many little curious or nice things were done away.[23]

The scene calls up in the mind the picture of Savonarola and the "burning of the vanities" in Renaissance Florence.

4

With this background of transatlantic Quaker thought and practice in mind, we may now inquire how far this esthetic of plainness governed the taste of the Quakers in colonial Philadelphia. In architecture and prose writing the influence is as obvious as the results were noteworthy. None of the eighteenth century Philadelphia meetinghouses is still standing, except that of the schismatic Free Quakers, but the Arch Street Meetinghouse, built in 1804, is fully representative of the type.[24] And within a radius of forty miles of the city one will find a score or more of the simpler country meetinghouses, erected before the American Revolution and still in use. With their clean lines and satisfying proportions, their paired entrances with modest door hoods, their simple rectangular floor plan with the characteristic sliding partition dividing the interior space into two equal rooms for the men's and women's business meetings they represent one of the most attractive and least-studied of early American architectural forms.[25] The typical literary expression of Quakerism is the

journal, or interior autobiography, of the Quaker minister or "[
Friend." The best-known example is, of course, John Wool
Journal, the masterpiece of the *genre,* but there were dozens of others,
each one reflecting in a somewhat stylized form the unique spiritual
experience of its author, and all of them written according to the
Quaker canons of the plain style.[26] But if one wishes to study the
Quaker esthetic at the point where its integral relationship to Quaker
life and thought is most clearly revealed, and all the stresses and
strains incident to the Quakers' involvement in the "world" are most
accurately recorded, one will focus one's attention on the minor arts.[27]

The number of craftsmen—joiners, turners, carvers, potters, glassmakers, pewterers, silversmiths—who came to William Penn's city
in the early, predominantly Quaker, migration was fairly large.[28] No
fewer than seventy-eight master craftsmen are known to have been
engaged in the woodworking trades alone before 1720, and of these
all but a handful were of the Friendly persuasion.[29] Quaker domina-
tion in these trades lasted long after the Friends had become a minority group in the Quaker City, lasted indeed through the highest
period of the Philadelphia Chippendale style. A surprising number
of the Philadelphia craftsmen who have become famous in recent
years and whose pieces are cherished by collectors and museums
were Quakers, including William Savery, Thomas Affleck, John
Letchworth, David Evans, the Claypooles. The brightest names
among the Philadelphia silversmiths and glassmakers—the Richard-
sons and Wistars—were also Quaker names. Unfortunately, we know
too little about these men. They were not poor, if we can judge by
the taxes they paid, but their annals are short and simple; in some
instances we have only their daybooks, giving the barest outlines of
their business transactions, and the records of their birth, marriage,
and death in the archives of the Quaker meetings. What their ideas
about their craft were we can only surmise, and imperfectly, from the
objects themselves.

We know more about their patrons, the great Quaker merchants,
who lived in their plain but comfortable mansions on Front Street
and Chestnut Street, who retired in the heat of the summer to their
country houses, or "plantations," on the outskirts of the town, and who
sent their ships, freighted with Pennsylvania produce or West India
goods or imported English wares into every port of the Atlantic

world. We know they formed a close-knit elite, which controlled the politics of the province as it dominated the economic and social life of the capital. We know a good deal about their reading habits, their humanitarian activities, their scientific interests. We know enough about them to realize that they formed a unique aristocracy, these Pembertons, Norrises, Logans, Dickinsons, Carpenters, Morrises, Drinkers, Whartons. For they were, after all, Quakers, members of a religious sect which preached a pure, spiritual religion, aloofness from the world, human equality in the sight of God, and, above all, simplicity. The demands of such a religion imposed severe strains on a prosperous and rising aristocracy; it created intolerable tensions, which some of them ultimately escaped by leaving the Society of Friends and joining the more fashionable, less demanding Church of England. For those who remained under the discipline of the meeting there was always the necessity of working out a practical compromise between the absolute spiritual and ethical demands of their faith and the strong pull of the world in which—socially, economically, politically—they were inextricably involved.

If they deviated from plainness by a jot or a tittle—or perhaps one should say by a boss or a finial—they stood under the judgment of their meeting, and had to face the disapproval, spoken and unspoken, of the simpler country Friends who, perhaps because they knew fewer of the temptations of the world, preserved the primitive Quaker ideal of simplicity more faithfully. As early as 1698 the Yearly Meeting of Women Friends was casting its disapproving eye into the interiors of certain Quaker homes in Philadelphia and warning "that no superfluous furniture be in your houses, as great fringes about your valances, and double valances, and double curtains, and many such-like needless things, which the Truth maketh manifest to the humble-minded."[30] Obviously there would have been no need to be quite so specific if some Friends were not actually furnishing their houses with these abominations. The earliest "book of discipline," issued in 1704 by Philadelphia Yearly Meeting, contained some strong words, quoted from London Yearly Meeting's epistle of the previous year:

And this Meeting, being under a deep sense that Pride [and] the vain Customs and fashions of the World Prevail over some under our profession, perticularly in the Excess of Apparel and furniture, doth earnestly rec-

ommend that all who make profession of the Truth take care to be ex-
amplary in what they wear and use, so as to avoid the vain Customs of the
World and all Extravagancy in colour and fashion. . . .[31]

The reiterated advices of the Yearly Meeting were reinforced by
the strictures of the traveling ministers from England and Ireland
and the other colonies who came to Philadelphia on religious visits,
and by the plain country Friends who came to town regularly to attend the sessions of the Yearly Meeting. The merchants usually enter-
tained these visitors in their houses, giving them an opportunity to
observe just how they lived. There are many hints in the journals of
the ministers that they found themselves uncomfortable and troubled
in the presence of the luxury they saw. John Woolman, of Mount
Holly, New Jersey, for example, often felt bound to labor with his
wealthy friends in the city to persuade them that their style of life
was out of keeping with Quaker plainness. This was a man so en-
amored of simplicity that when he observed "sundry sorts of Carved
work and Imagery" outside the cabin of a ship in which he had taken
passage to England, and "some superfluity of workmanship of several
sorts" inside the cabin, he insisted on traveling steerage so that his
eye would not fall on these extravagances![32] One can imagine his
state of mind in the presence of an elaborately carved Affleck or
Savery highboy.

In 1764, an elderly country Friend, John Smith of Chester County,
stood up in the Yearly Meeting of Ministers and Elders and reviewed
the history of Philadelphia Quakerism as he had observed it in his
lifetime. In the early years of the century, he recalled, "Friends were
a plain, lowly minded people and . . . there was much tenderness
and Contrition in their meetings." But after twenty years or so, "the
society increasing in wealth and in some degree conforming to the
fashions of the World, true Humility decreased and their meetings
in general were not so lively and Edifying." By the end of forty years,
he said, "many of the Society were grown rich; that wearing of fine
costly garments and with fashionable furniture, silver watches became customary with many. . . ." And as these customs prevailed,
he lamented, "so the powerful overshadowings of the Holy Spirit
were less manifested among us."[33] In this analysis, with its suggestion
of an inverse relationship between spiritual vitality and such indices

of worldliness as fashionable furniture and silver watches, speaks the authentic voice of traditional plain Quakerism.

Clearly the Quaker merchants, the objects of this criticism, were furnishing their houses with the finest products of the Quaker craftsmen. The daybooks of Joseph Richardson, at the Historical Society of Pennsylvania, for example, are full of names of the Quaker merchant princes. Many of the best pieces of colonial furniture that have come down to us—the work of Savery and Affleck and Evans—originally stood in the homes of the Quaker grandees of Front Street and Chestnut Street. Even if one doubted the ascriptions and provenances of these pieces, there is the independent testimony of that inquisitive and observant Scandinavian, Professor Peter Kalm, who noted in the middle of the century that "the more well-to-do [Friends] employ only Quaker artisans if they can be found."[34] A few surviving pieces of furniture from the earliest years of Pennsylvania seem to reveal a conscious and conscientious striving for simplicity, a deliberate stripping away of superfluities. There is, for example, a chair said to have belonged to William Penn himself, which is described by W. M. Hornor as "a plain version of the elaborate Stuart pattern."[35] And several of the pieces which Penn's chief American representative, James Logan, had at Stenton, his country seat north of Philadelphia, have the same character. The Logan furniture now at the Historical Society of Pennsylvania is exemplary in its plainness. Basically, the pieces are William and Mary and Queen Anne designs, but they are almost completely lacking in ornamentation. In this respect they matched the house in which they stood. Stenton, the Logan mansion, is a superb example of early Georgian in basic design and proportions. But it is almost wholly lacking in the distinctive Georgian vocabulary of decorative details—pediments, columns, pilasters, Palladian windows, and the rest. Comparison with the equally lovely but much more showy mansion which William Byrd built at the same period at Westover clearly reveals the distance between the sophisticated taste of a Virginia gentleman and the principled plainness of the Quaker merchant.

The identifiable furniture of the next generation of Quaker merchants—the generation which spanned the middle years of the eighteenth century—seems to show a growing accommodation to the world: it is much more ornately carved and richly elaborated. To some extent, no doubt, this simply reflects the transition from the relative simplicity of Queen Anne to the rococo intricacies of Chippendale. One might be tempted to say on the basis of the surviving evidence that the taste of this generation of Quaker merchants was not markedly different from that of the non-Quakers with whom they now shared social and economic preeminence. And one would not be wholly wrong. The chairs and highboys, the tankards and tea services which Savery and Affleck and Richardson made for their Quaker customers do not seem to be noticeably plainer than those they made for the Philadelphia gentlemen who worshiped on Sundays at Christ Church or St. Peter's.

Of course, the surviving evidence is inevitably incomplete, and therefore may be deceptive. After all, the examples of Philadelphia craftsmanship which have caught the connoisseur's eye and been preserved in museums naturally tend to be the more spectacular pieces. Many of the more typical products fashioned by Quaker craftsmen for their Quaker clients may have disappeared. There is written evidence to support the perfectly reasonable speculation that the average wealthy Quaker household was furnished in a special kind of plainness. It suggests that the Quaker merchants found a rationale by which they could satisfy their human urge toward conspicuous consumption without falling under the ban of the meeting.

In 1707 Joseph Pike, the Irish Friend whom we last saw taking down his curiously carved mouldings, disposing of his fine veneered cabinets, and cutting the fringe off his valances, wrote to Isaac Norris, one of the great merchants of early Philadelphia, reproaching him and his family for departing from plainness in their dress and house furnishings as they rose in the world. Norris, in reply, admitted that he and his family were beginning to live in some style and comfort. He agreed that on the whole it was safer to err on the side of self-denial than of self-indulgence. Still, he said, he could not consider it reasonable that a man of substance and station should "wear the same and live at the same rate within-doors" as an ordinary artisan or yeoman farmer. "Every man," he thought, "ought soberly and discreetly to set bounds to himself and avoid extremes, *still bearing due regard to the society he is of*."[36] In other words, plainness was a relative matter in a graded society in which some men were obviously poor and humble and others by God's grace and their own efforts wealthy and prominent.

Plainness could be manifested by a studied avoidance of gaudy or overelaborate ornamentation. But there was nothing in the Quaker discipline that proscribed fine materials or sound workmanship or harmonious proportions; and evidence is plentiful that the Quaker merchants took this way of satisfying their hunger for esthetic pleasure as well as their desire for the conspicuous display of wealth appropriate to their station in the world. The inventory of Jonathan Dickinson's household goods as early as 1722 shows that most of his furniture was of mahogany.[37] Christopher Sower, the German printer, observed in 1724 that the Quakers still dressed plainly "except that the material is very costly, or is even velvet."[38] In 1738 John Reynell ordered from London "a Handsome plain Looking-Glass . . . and 2 raised Japan'd Black Corner Cubbards, with 2 Doors to each, no Red in 'em, of the best Sort but Plain."[39] In that phrase—"of the best Sort but Plain"—lies the Quaker merchant's practical resolution of the conflict between his Quaker instincts and his sense of his status in society. There is much more evidence to the same effect. Peter Kalm, a dozen years later, reported that although the Quakers "pretend not to have their clothes made after the latest fashion, or to wear cuffs and be dressed as gaily as others, they strangely enough have their garments made of the finest and costliest materials that can be procured."[40] And the French traveler Brissot noticed in 1788 that the furniture in Quaker houses had "the appearance of simplicity; but in many instances it is certainly expensive."[41]

5

Because Quakerism, as I said at the beginning, was fundamentally a way of life rather than a system of thought or scheme of doctrines, it follows that any crisis in the Quaker conscience was sure to be reflected in the merchants' manner of living. Such a crisis of conscience occurred in the Society of Friends in Pennsylvania in the years just before and during the American Revolution. It is not necessary here to explore in detail the causes of that crisis. It will be enough to say that the coming of Indian war to the borders of the colony in 1755, the year of Braddock's defeat, brought an end to the seventy-five-year

reign of peace in the colony. It was the signal for the Quakers to ab-
dicate their places of political power. The Holy Experiment was over:
it had ended in failure. The downfall of the "peaceable kingdom" was
announced by the shrieks of inflamed Indians and the sharp reports
of frontiersmen's rifles. The hostilities against the mother country
which engulfed all the colonies twenty years later, after Lexington
and Concord, only deepened the crisis. These tragic events caused the
Quakers, and especially the Philadelphia merchants, to reexamine the
whole tenor of their lives. How did their professions of plainness, of
primitive, apostolic simplicity, square with their practice, with their
comfortable, aristocratic existence in their splendidly furnished Philadelphia mansions and their handsome country estates? The searching
words of the saintly John Woolman suddenly came home to them:
"May we look upon our Treasures, and the furniture of our Houses,
and the Garments in which we array ourselves, and try whether the
seeds of war have nourishment in these our possessions. . . ."[42]

Philadelphia Quakerism underwent a thoroughgoing "reformation" in the Revolutionary era.[43] The scenes enacted in Irish Quaker
homes in the 1690's in the time of Joseph Pike were reenacted in
Philadelphia Quaker houses, as committees of concerned Friends
went from family to family, laboring with each one to put away its
fripperies and superfluities and restore the ancient simplicity of
Truth. Those who resisted, who refused to give up their gay sashes
and rich laces, their exquisite carved chests and elegant tea services,
had to listen to stern jeremiads from more "consistent" Friends like
Anthony Benezet. If they faltered, if they clung to the "world," they
stood in danger ultimately of disownment, of ejection from the household of the faith. It is symbolic that the son of William Savery, who
came of age just before the Revolution, did not follow his father's
calling, but was apprenticed to a tanner and was later recorded as a
Quaker minister. His great triumph was not to have created beautiful
examples of the cabinetmaker's art but to have converted a high-
spirited English girl named Betsy Gurney from the world of high
fashion and to have set her on the road of plainness and good works
which led her, as Elizabeth Fry, in drab gown and plain bonnet,
to spend herself ministering to the wretched inmates of Newgate
Prison.[44]

By the end of the eighteenth century, as a result of a drastic purg-

ing and pruning, the Philadelphia Friends, except for a few unrecon-
structed worldlings, known in their time as "wet Quakers," had become as plain as those on the other side of the Atlantic. The classic
description of the plain Quaker way of life was set down in 1806 by
Thomas Clarkson in his *Portraiture of Quakerism*. Though he was
writing of English Friends, his observations apply equally well to
the Philadelphia Quakers in the early days of the Republic. Their
choice of furniture, he said, like their choice of clothes, was "governed
by the rules of decency and usefulness, but never by the suggestions
of shew. The adoption of taste instead of utility," he went on, ". . .
would be considered as a conscious conformity with the fashions of the
world." The few Quakers who were poor, of course, had no choice but
to use "homely furniture." The middle-class Friends likewise had the
habit of plainness. "As to the rich," he admitted,

there is a difference in the practice of these. Some, and indeed many of
them, use as plain and frugal furniture, as those in moderate circumstances.
Others again step beyond the practice of the middle classes, and buy what
is more costly, not with a view of shew so much as to accommodate their
furniture to the size and goodness of their houses. In the houses of others
again, who have more than ordinary intercourse with the world, we now
and then see what is elegant, but seldom what would be considered to be
extravagant furniture. We see no chairs with satin bottoms and gilded
frames, no magnificent pier-glasses, no superb chandeliers, no curtains
with extravagant trimmings. . . . If there are persons in the society, who
use them, they must be few in number, and these must be conscious that,
by the introduction of such finery into their houses . . . they are . . .
departing from the spirit of Quakerism.[45]

The essential spirit of Quakerism may have been antiesthetic in
its fear of the "world," its scorn of the sensuous, the merely ornamental. Certainly it ran counter to the baroque taste of the seventeenth century as it ran counter to the rococo taste of the eighteenth.
But in any style as extravagant as the baroque or the rococo, there is
always the danger that the ornamental may become the meretricious.
Perhaps in some measure we owe to the religious instincts of the
Quaker merchants and artisans the unfailing soundness of workmanship and sureness of line that characterize the best Philadelphia
craftsmanship of the eighteenth century. In any case "the simplicity
of Truth" is no unworthy esthetic ideal in itself.

CHAPTER VI

Quietism Versus Enthusiasm:
The Philadelphia Quakers
and the Great Awakening

The Inward Light is still the central and distinctive, perhaps the only, doctrine held by all members of the Society of Friends—by "conservative" and "liberal" Quakers, rural and urban Quakers, English-speaking Quakers and German-speaking Quakers, white Quakers in Philadelphia and black Quakers in Kenya. The inward message which George Fox knew does not change—"Jesus Christ the same yesterday, today, and forever"—but the way in which the message is received does change; and the changes are in large measure conditioned by the adjacent culture and the extent to which the Friends have accommodated themselves to it. The degree of accommodation, indeed the very aspects of the culture with which they are in contact, will depend in part on their social status.

The earliest Friends, by and large, came from the lower classes, or at most from the emerging *petite bourgeoisie* in England. They were simple husbandmen or yeoman farmers from the countryside or artisans from the towns. (George Fox himself was a weaver's son and had been apprenticed to a shoemaker.) In this stratum of society the highly emotional species of religious experience which contemporaries called *enthusiasm* was indigenous. A century later, however, economic success had carried the Quakers of Philadelphia up to the topmost rung of the social ladder: they were the aristocrats of the colonial social order, and their religious experience was colored by their sense of the behavior proper to their social position. At the same time, by institutionalizing their religious testimonies, they had built

91

a hedge around their community, thereby insulating themselves in a measure from the life around them. Thus, when George Whitefield, the evangelist of the "Great Awakening," came from England, bringing a mighty renewal of religious enthusiasm to the Quaker City, the Friends stood aside and watched disapprovingly as the fires of America's first great religious revival raged around them. Social and cultural change within the Society of Friends had brought with it a striking alteration in the very nature of Quaker spiritual experience, from "enthusiasm" to "quietism," from a prophetic to a more mystical type of religion.[1]

But no cultural hedge is impermeable, nor does cultural change ever cease. A century after the Great Awakening, the Friends who had moved westward with the moving frontier and found themselves in the raw new society of Kansas and Iowa and Oregon, were caught up in the excitement of a revivalistic religion that had become endemic in western America. As the western Friends acquired the revival habit, they gradually—some groups more than others—took over other characteristics from the evangelical churches—a paid ministry, the singing of hymns, a fundamentalist theology, even in some cases the use of the sacraments (which the early Friends had abandoned), and became known as the "Friends Church."

On the east coast and in England, meanwhile, this particular accommodation to culture did not take place, but equally significant and far-reaching changes were in the making. The late nineteenth century saw the first generation of college- and university-educated Quakers. (Haverford School became a college, authorized to grant degrees, in 1856; Swarthmore College was founded in 1864; and the doors of the English universities were opened to Friends in 1871.) Consequently, Quakerism in the twentieth century tended to take on an intellectual cast, very different from the character of the early movement, when George Fox had fulminated against the universities as the enemies of true religion. Most of the new Quaker meetings established in the past twenty-five years have actually been in university towns. Along with this development has gone a noticeable shift in the occupational status of Friends—away from farming and small business into the intellectual professions, into teaching, research, social work, medicine, the law—and a concomitant change in the conception, if not in the actual experience, of the Inward Light

—a tendency to identify it, on the one hand, with man's rational faculty and, on the other, to return to a purely mystical basis.

All these changes represent differential adjustments to culture among a people who still count themselves "children of the Light." No one has yet explored these changes thoroughly, though an understanding of them would obviously illuminate many of the problems of religion and culture. The following chapter seeks to analyze the relationship at a particular time and place—Philadelphia in the exciting period of the Great Awakening.

In a well-known passage in his *Autobiography* Benjamin Franklin describes his reaction to the perfervid preaching of George Whitefield, the foremost evangelist of the Great Awakening. The passage is usually cited as an illustration of the emotional susceptibility of the eighteenth century man of reason:

I happened [writes Franklin] . . . to attend one of his sermons, in the course of which I perceived he intended to finish with a collection, and I silently resolved he should get nothing from me. I had in my pocket a handful of copper money, three or four silver dollars, and five pistoles in gold. As he proceeded I began to soften, and concluded to give the coppers. Another stroke of his oratory made me asham'd of that, and determin'd me to give the silver; and he finish'd so admirably, that I empty'd my pocket wholly into the collector's dish, gold and all.

The remainder of the passage, often overlooked, is not without interest, for it draws attention to the one important group in Philadelphia which was proof against Whitefield's appeal to emotion:

At this sermon there was also one of our club, who, being of my sentiments . . . and suspecting a collection might be intended, had, by precaution, emptied his pockets before he came from home. Towards the conclusion of the discourse, however, he felt a strong desire to give, and apply'd to a neighbour, who stood near him, to borrow some money for the purpose. The application was unfortunately [made] to perhaps the only man in the company who had the firmness not to be affected by the preacher. His answer was, *"At any other time, Friend Hopkinson, I would lend to thee freely; but not now, for thee seems to be out of thy right senses."*[2]

The conclusion of this incident, when noted at all, has usually been regarded simply as a reflection of the parsimony associated in the popular mind with Quakers. Actually, as this essay will attempt to demonstrate, it reflects something more significant, and sheds some light on the nature and development of popular religious movements. It is fortunately possible to document the reaction of Philadelphia Quakerdom to the Great Awakening by means of passages from contemporary letters and journals. After a comparison of the basic doctrines of Quakerism and Evangelicalism as expounded by their leading spokesmen, a hypothesis will be offered to explain the attitude which the Philadelphia Quakers exhibited in the face of the revival.

1

By 1739, when George Whitefield first appeared in Philadelphia, the Quaker movement was nearly a century old. It had left behind it the ardors and extravagances of its primitive period. No longer as in the days of George Fox and James Nayler were Friends reviled as wild enthusiasts and hysterical fanatics; no longer were they thrown into jail as heretics, firebrands, and disturbers of the peace. With the advent of toleration, the passing of the first-generation leaders, and the adoption of birthright membership, they had settled into a period characterized by a less prophetic ministry, a more introspective mysticism, and a fear of "creaturely activity." Their religion had become a matter of quiet waiting on the Lord "in the silence of the flesh." There was in this quietism no trace of the ethical antinomianism of European Quietism, nor did it by any means tend to inhibit action, as the careers of John Woolman and Anthony Benezet bear eloquent witness. Nevertheless it made Friends hypercautious lest they "outrun their Guide," and it fostered a distrust of actions too lightly undertaken "in the will of the creature."[3]

Not only had Friends become reserved and introverted religiously; they had also become socially respectable. The early Friends had been recruited largely from the lower strata of society, from among the artisans, shopkeepers, domestic servants, yeoman farmers, and husbandmen of Commonwealth and Restoration England. By the practice of the economic virtues of diligence, prudence, and thrift, they had risen in the course of years to the status of substantial and respected upper-middle-class citizens. A little aloof, perhaps, from "the world" and its follies, preserving their character as a "peculiar people" by certain singularities of dress and address, they had attained, both in England and in the colonies, to a secure place in the upper ranks of society. In Philadelphia, whither they had migrated a half-century earlier as craftsmen, shopkeepers, and small farmers, they now constituted a mercantile aristocracy, sharing their social position only with the more fashionable Anglicans.

The full impact of the Great Awakening reached Philadelphia late in 1739 with the arrival of George Whitefield from England. It is not necessary here to expatiate upon the nature of this extraordinary revival of religion or to trace its wildfire course through the Middle Colonies. It is sufficient to say that throughout eastern Pennsylvania and New Jersey, as earlier in New England and somewhat later in the southern colonies, religion replaced the weather for a season as the normal topic of conversation, and the question on nearly everyone's lips was "What must I do to be saved?" Even so detached an observer as Benjamin Franklin was impressed by the reformation in Philadelphia. "It was wonderful," he wrote, "to see the change soon made in the manners of our inhabitants. From being thoughtless or indifferent about religion, it seem'd as if all the world were growing religious, so that one could not walk thro' the town in an evening without hearing psalms sung in different families of every street."[4]

The young George Whitefield, fresh from his evangelistic triumphs among the Kingswood colliers and the London rabble, was the head and front of the revival. Ably abetted by local pulpit orators like Gilbert Tennent, he preached the depravity of man, the necessity of conversion, and the ineffable bliss of salvation, with such power that thousands were converted and professed their faith in Jesus Christ. The revival transcended denominational lines, injecting a new emotional fervor into the religious life of Presbyterians, Baptists, Lutherans, Dutch Reformed, and German Reformed alike. From the aristocratic Anglicans at one end of the social scale to the unchurched masses at the other, the flames of the revival leaped, bringing the religious life of the region to a white heat. Only the Society of Friends remained insulated against the fires of religious emotionalism that were sweeping the countryside.

2

Two brief scenes on shipboard provide a sort of preview of later relations between the Friends and the revivalists in Philadelphia. One of Whitefield's fellow travelers on the voyage to America in the autumn of 1739 was a Quaker minister, and Whitefield demonstrated his characteristic freedom from sectarian narrowness by turning his cabin over to the Quaker for religious meetings: ". . . gave a Quaker preacher (at his desire) the use of my cabin in the afternoon," he records in his journal for September 5, 1739. "He spoke chiefly concerning the false pretences and education of those who run before they are called of God into the ministry of the Church of England. Woe be unto those who give the adversaries cause thus to speak reproachfully of us."[5]

Here was an echo of what the Lord had "opened" to George Fox a century before as he wandered about the midlands of England: "that being bred at Oxford or Cambridge was not enough to fit and qualify men to be ministers of Christ."[6] It was an affirmation to which Whitefield and the other Evangelical leaders could subscribe, for although they did not disparage theological education, they nevertheless acknowledged in common with the Quakers that the Gospel could be acceptably preached by unlearned men and that the fundamental qualification for the ministry was not an academic degree but a divine call.

A few weeks later, when Whitefield again lent his cabin to the Quaker, a basic cleavage between their religious views manifested itself. The Quaker "spoke with much earnestness," wrote Whitefield, "but in my opinion his foundation was wrong. He seemed to make the light of conscience and the Holy Spirit one and the same thing, and represented Christ *within,* and not Christ *without* as the foundation of our faith: whereas the outward righteousness of Jesus Christ imputed to us, I believe, is the sole fountain and cause of all inward communications which we receive from the Spirit of God."[7]

The fundamental theological divergence between Quakerism and Evangelicalism is here laid bare. The Quaker characteristically emphasized the inward working of the Holy Spirit, the Christ formed in man's soul, whereas the Evangelical rested his faith on the objective historic Christ and His vicarious atonement. The eighteenth century Friends indeed laid less stress on external factors or "outward helps" in religion than George Fox had done, and it was natural that Whitefield should be shocked by their concern with the Christ within almost to the exclusion of the historic Christ. This proved to be a continual stumbling block to Whitefield in his relations with the Quakers. On his second day in Philadelphia he attended Friends' meeting and, as he puts it, "felt somewhat in sympathy with the man that spoke. But," he adds, "I heartily wish that they would talk of an outward as well as an inward Christ."[8]

Whitefield disembarked at Lewes, Delaware, and proceeded at once to Philadelphia, arriving there on November 3, 1739. Friends in Philadelphia shared in the general interest and curiosity which greeted his long-heralded coming. A prominent Quaker merchant, writing to his London correspondent on the day after Whitefield's arrival, took occasion in a letter otherwise devoted to business matters to note: "Whitefield preached today in the church belonging to this city to a large audience, and is to do the like tomorrow."[9] James Pemberton, member of the leading Quaker family of Philadelphia, noted his popularity a week later (November 11) but reserved judgment on his preaching:

He preaches every day. Some of our curious youth of rash judgment, who look at words more than substance, are very constant in attendance and much pleased. He preached three nights successively upon our Court House steps, on Second Street, where he exceedingly takes with the people. . . . His intentions are good, but he has not yet arrived at such perfection as to see as far as he yet may.[10]

On his successive visits to Philadelphia during the next few years, Whitefield continued to be a subject of discussion among Friends. His journals disclose that he often visited Friends in their homes, and sometimes attended their meetings for worship.

The typical Quaker attitude toward the revival at its outset was compounded of an aloof but tolerant amusement at the antics of the preachers and a somewhat grudging admiration for their success in mending the morals of the Philadelphians. John Smith, a cultivated young Friend of Burlington, New Jersey, soon to enter the mercantile society of Philadelphia, took an intelligent, though detached, interest in the progress of the revival and the theological controversies in which Whitefield became engaged. He bought Whitefield's journals as they came in successive installments from Franklin's press and took pains to inform himself upon the doctrinal issues raised by his preaching.[11] As a good Quaker, however, he regarded "notions" about predestination and the relative efficacy of faith and works as inessential and barren concomitants of religion. In April, 1740, he writes in a vein of tolerant urbanity:

We hear from Philadelphia that George Whitefield is arrived there and preaches daily to great numbers of people. Last First Day morning before church time he preached a sermon on faith in opposition to the doctrine of good works being absolutely necessary to our justification in the sight of God. And at church (so called) their parson Commings preached up works in opposition to Whitefield, and in the evening Whitefield again preached in opposition to him. So that those of the black robe sometimes display their different opinions.[12]

On another Philadelphia Friend, Whitefield's preaching made a more positive impression. Richard Hockley, a member of the mercantile aristocracy, wrote on June 8, 1740, to a London correspondent:

I can't pass over in silence to you the surprising change and alteration I see in the people of this place since that shining light the Reverend Mr. Whitefield has been amongst them whom no doubt you have heard of; religion is the topic of conversation, and they all have it so much in their mouths, pray God it may sink deep into their hearts so as to influence their actions and conversation, make them good neighbors and sincere friends, which I know you will say Amen to. I have heard him several times here and in South Carolina, and had several private conversations with him. He appears to me to be a very sincere person, zealous for his Master's cause, and justly admired for his elegant though plain language and easy to be understood, and for the serious vein of piety that runs through all his exhortations, crowded after by multitudes, though much traduced by some who have no true sense of religion. He is endeavoring to reclaim a wicked, vicious, and sinful age, and that with great authority and courage, and [I] must own to you I never heard of or saw his fellow.[13]

Hockley later came to alter his opinion of Whitefield, finding his rigid predestinarianism unpalatable. Two years later, while the revival was still in progress, he wrote to another correspondent:

I . . . am steadfast to the Quakers' principles which I have always professed, and like[d] Mr. Whitefield when he preached them up until he derogated from them and got into the scheme of reprobation which by no means squares with the notions that I hold after a mature and deliberate consideration of the means of salvation through Christ.[14]

A handful of Friends, carried away by the impassioned preaching of Whitefield and his fellow evangelists, turned their backs upon their Quaker inheritance and embraced the more exciting religious life which the Great Awakening introduced into the colonies. Benjamin Franklin considered it an event worthy of being brought to the attention of the readers of his newspaper when on May 31, 1741, Gilbert Tennent "baptised at the New-Building Eight adult Persons, who had been of the People called Quakers, one, as is said, a Preacher."[15] Whitefield indeed boasted: "Many of the Quakers have been convinced of the righteousness of Jesus Christ and openly confess the truth as it is in Jesus: for which I believe they will shortly be put out of their synagogues. Some of their head men are zealous against me, and are much afraid their foundation will be sadly shaken."[16] There is no evidence, however, that any significant number of Friends were torn away from their traditional moorings.[17]

As the revival progressed, the attitude of most Friends, following the pattern set by that of Richard Hockley, tended to become one of ill-concealed disapproval and quiet hostility. In May, 1740, for example, Judah Foulke, a Philadelphia Friend, wrote to John Smith in Burlington:

Our town is in an uproar about this Whitefield. For my part I once had a good opinion of the man, but I am afraid he has let his zeal carry him too far in some things, in pulling down the writings of them who are dead and not here to vindicate their own cause, which seems to have too much self and bigotry, to pull down other[s] and set up himself. . . . This won't end here, I am afraid, for some of his followers begin to come forth in the

same manner and preach the same doctrine as he does. By the time that
he comes again, they intend to build him a church—and then our foundations will be tried.[18]

The attitude of James Logan, erstwhile secretary to William Penn
and now the most distinguished citizen of provincial Pennsylvania,
passed through the same successive stages, and his reaction may be
taken as a representative Quaker view of the revival in Philadelphia:

None can be long a stranger to George Whitefield. All I have to say of
him is, that by good language, a better utterance, an engaging manner,
and a powerful voice, he gained much at first on most sorts of people. . . .
It must be confessed his preaching has a good effect in reclaiming many
dissolute people, but from his countenancing so very much the most hot-
headed predestinarians, and those of them, principally, who had been accounted by the more sober as little better than madmen, he and they have
actually driven divers into despair, and some into perfect madness. In short,
it is apprehended by the more judicious that the whole will end in confusion, to the great prejudice of the cause of virtue and solid religion; his
doctrine turning on the danger of good works without such a degree of
sanctifying faith as comes up to his gauge.[19]

It will be noted that, along with the predestinarianism and solifid-
ianism of the revival preachers, it was the emotional excesses and
the psychological disorders which they induced that most disturbed
Logan. An exchange of letters between John Smith and James Pemberton is highly revealing in this connection for it gives us a hint
of what was, perhaps, the fundamental cause of the coolness of the
Quakers toward the revival. The discussion was touched off by the
publication in the *American Weekly Mercury* of a "Letter from a
Gentleman of East Lyme, in Connecticut, to the Rev. Mr. Gilbert
Tennent of New Brunswick." It describes in vivid terms the extraordinary outburst of revival spirit which followed in the wake of
Gilbert Tennent's visit to New England in the winter of 1740–1741:
"it's a most blessed Time," writes this rhapsodic correspondent,
"it's a mere Heaven upon Earth, the People from dull carelessness,
now are like the Horse-leach at the Vein, crying give, give." It was
the following description of the emotional extravagances and the
religious hysteria accompanying the revival which particularly attracted the shocked attention of the two Friends:

there has scarcely been a Sermon preached, but some Persons were deeply Wounded, and many removed out of the House, Fainting and Swooning, the Children of all Ages from 6 Years old and upwards are great sharers in this blessed Work, and talk most wonderfully of the Things of God, the great and unwearied Pains they take to bring their Mates to CHRIST with them is a standing reproach to these that are grown up.[20]

James Pemberton, reading of these pentecostal scenes, was moved to write to John Smith:

Thou hast doubtless seen that wonderful letter in the last *Mercury* setting forth the great reformation and outcries in New England (the product of G.T.'s doctrine). I believe it has proceeded more from the terrifying expressions of some of their teachers there than [from] any real sense of a true hearty religion, which by all accounts had a very different effect at the first appearance of our worthy Friends, who suffered so many cruelties for the advancement of that blessed Truth now too little noticed by too many of this generation; but indeed there are so few good examples of true piety in this day. . . . Oh, that there were many more! but it being now a time of ease, people have not so much to rouse them as formerly.[21]

John Smith's reply deserves quotation *in extenso* no less for the remarkable reproduction of the more horrendous sort of eighteenth century revival sermon, than for the detached, almost rationalistic, explanation of its effects:

I exactly agree with thee in opinion concerning the wonderful letter in the last *Mercury*.

I reckon among all the delusions of the notionists it is not the least, that of pretending and publishing that great numbers of children of six years old and upwards are brought under deep convictions, nay, are converted by their ministry.

I have seen a boy younger imitate a preacher very nicely, use unexceptionable words, and deliver himself as if he was affected with what he said—but I count it no miracle.

Who does not know that children of that age, by example and tuition, are capable of imitating almost anything?

It is not possible to think that they, seeing their parents and other grown people making hideous noises and violent distortions of the body, might by nature be prompted to do the like?

We see it common in children much younger, when they see others cry, they will do the same. Every like begets its like; so if they chance to see a frightful sight, how dismally will they shriek and cry out!

Now what can appear more dreadful to their childish apprehensions than being told a dreadful burning Tophet, an eternal Hell, scorching, blazing, fiery brimstone ready to overtake them, sure damnation, certain destruction and unavoidable desolation, where they must forever dwell with devils, fallen angels, damned spirits, fiery furies, forever burning, tormenting, and never, never, to be released?

I say, what can be more terrifying than this? And I think when we consider that these are their frequent and familiar expressions, we need not be surprised at the outcries made by children, *etc.*

Even a parrot may be taught to speak some few words, but he cannot give any rational account of the cause of those words. Why? Because he is destitute of the power of reflection and so incapable of understanding the difference between causes and their effects.[22]

These comments unconsciously reveal a good deal about the course of popular religious movements. Here are the heirs of one movement of uninhibited emotional religion pronouncing judgment from the vantage point of a century-long development into emotional restraint and social respectability upon a cognate movement of vital popular religion in the first flush of its exuberant youth. The relatively sophisticated Quaker of the eighteenth century looked upon the excesses of religious frenzy produced by the revival with distaste, forgetting, even denying, that his seventeenth century forebears had allowed their religious emotions to express themselves with equal abandon and equal scorn for the norms of civilized behavior. Without realizing it, Pemberton put his finger upon the social fact which in large measure explained the transformation of Quakerism from enthusiasm to quietism: "it being now a time of ease, people have not so much to rouse them as formerly." John Greenleaf Whittier, whose historical insights are often more remarkable than his poetry, reached the same conclusion in "The Preacher," a poem based on the career of George Whitefield:

> With zeal wing-clipped and white-heat cool,
> Moved by the spirit in grooves of rule,
> No longer harried, and cropped, and fleeced,
> Flogged by sheriff and cursed by priest,

But by wiser counsels left at ease
To settle quietly on his lees,
And, self-concentred, to count as done
The work which his fathers well begun,
In silent protest of letting alone,
The Quaker kept the way of his own,
A non-conductor among the wires,
With coat of asbestos proof to fires.
And quite unable to mend his pace
To catch the falling manna of grace,
He hugged the closer his little store
Of faith, and silently prayed for more.

As for the conversion of children, which John Smith counted among the "delusions of the notionists," it was doubtless unheard of among eighteenth century Friends, but it had not always been so. Robert Barclay testifies that in the seventeenth century the Lord's power "would sometimes also reach to and wonderfully work even in little children, to the admiration and astonishment of many."[23] The Quaker school at Waltham Abbey in England, for example, had in 1679 been the scene of a remarkable religious revival:

God's heavenly power broke forth in some young girls; [runs a contemporary account] it began with three or four at first, broke them into tears and melting of heart, then reached two or three of the younger boys, and in a very small time reached all the children, many of them being from eight to ten years old; the power was so mighty, that they were all broken into tears, some into trembling, and at last it spread unto the elder people; and continued about one hour, until the meeting ended.[24]

One final incident may be cited to illustrate the growth of hostility among Friends toward the revival. It occurred in an evening meeting for worship in October, 1741, and is recorded in the journal of Benjamin Ferris:

after we had sat in silence a while there came into the meeting a very mean priest to look at, and I believe he was so too; for he went right along up into the gallery, I think, with his hat under his arm, and as soon as he got up into the gallery, he fell to praying, the meeting all keeping their seats, none rising up for his pretended worship to the Lord. He soon concluded his prayer and began to preach, but not being suffered to preach there, he sat down and sat still; and after a while Robert Jordan stood up and preached, showing the difference between the teachings of the spirit of God and that proceeding from the enemy, or from man's wisdom, and the difference between ministering from the gift of God or the will of man, which he spoke livingly of and in a true sense, and concluded the meeting with prayer, the forward priest kneeling down also on his knees in the time of prayer. The meeting ended in quietness.[25]

In Robert Jordan spoke the voice of Quaker quietism. According to the Quaker view, the only true ministry was that of the Spirit making use of human instruments; words uttered in the will or wisdom of man were of no spiritual value. But one catches a note of uncharitableness in the intimation that the preaching of the intruder—undoubtedly one of the wandering evangelists spawned by the revival—proceeded from the Devil; and one cannot avoid the inference that the "mean" (that is, poor, shabby) appearance of the preacher had something to do with his chilly reception. The time had been, of course, when the early Friends—the "First Publishers of Truth"—had been just such peripatetic exhorters, mean in appearance and forward in manner. The aversion with which Friends greeted the intrusion of this stranger is the measure of the change which had overtaken Quakerism since its earliest days, when George Fox and his colleagues had unceremoniously entered the "steeple-houses" of England to set forth their heterodox and unwelcome views. This was not the first time in religious history that members of a church have failed to recognize their ancestors when they have appeared in their midst.

3

Throughout this essay the existence of a common element in Quakerism and Evangelicalism has been implicitly assumed. It is time to make this assumption explicit. That which the two movements had in common was a central persuasion that God reveals Himself directly to individual men through the Holy Spirit. The historical function of both movements in their time was to shift the basis of religious authority from outward belief to inward experience, from intellectual assent to experiential certainty.

"Though I read the Scriptures that spoke of Christ and God," wrote George Fox, "yet I knew him not, but by revelation, as he who hath the key did open, and as the Father of life drew me to his Son by his spirit."[26] The Quakers made a vital distinction between what Barclay called "the certain knowledge of God and the uncertain; betwixt the spiritual knowledge and the literal; the saving heart-knowledge and the soaring, airy head-knowledge." This last, he confessed, "may be divers ways obtained; but the first, by no other way than the inward immediate manifestation and revelation of God's spirit shining in and upon the heart, enlightening and opening the understanding."[27]

The doctrine of immediate inspiration was no less characteristic of the Evangelical movement. "Every good gift is from God," wrote John Wesley, "and is given to man by the Holy Ghost. . . . The natural man discerneth not the things of the Spirit of God; so that we can never discern them until God reveals them unto us by His Spirit."[28] The ultimate source of authority in religious matters for the Evangelicals was the witness of the Spirit which Wesley defined as "an inward impression on the soul, whereby the Spirit of God directly witnesses to my spirit that I am a child of God."[29] By no means minimizing the importance of the objective doctrines and ordinances of historical Christianity, the leaders of the Evangelical movement, in protest against the growth of deism and rationalism, laid primary emphasis upon the inner experience of religion, an emphasis which brought a new warmth of vital piety into English and American religious life.

George Whitefield, though he differed with Wesley on theological grounds (clinging to an obsolescent Calvinism in contrast to the Arminianism of Wesley), shared his faith in immediate inspiration. He was conscious of "extraordinary communications" or divine impulses which were self-authenticating and infallible. This caused him to be suspect in the eyes of most orthodox Protestants for whom revelation had ceased with the final "Amen" of the Apocalypse. Isaac Watts, the Nonconformist theologian and hymn writer, wrote of him in 1739:

I wish Mr. Whitefield would not have risen above any pretences to the ordinary influences of the Holy Spirit unless he could have given some better evidences of it. He has acknowledged to me in conversation that he knows an impression on his mind to be divine, though he cannot give me any convincing proofs of it.[30]

Whitefield recognized his agreement with the Quakers on this point. Just before his departure for America in 1739, he held several meetings with English Friends, and although he disapproved of their attitude toward tithes and sacraments, he admitted that "their notions about walking and being led by the Spirit were right and good."[31] His adversaries in America were not slow to tax him with reviving the heresy of the Quakers. Charles Chauncy, leading spokesman of the "opposers" of the revival in New England, referred to him in 1743 as "Quakerish," and an Old Side Presbyterian pamphlet entitled *The Querists* objected to his reference to Christ's being spiritually formed in men's hearts as equivalent to Barclay's doctrine of the Christ Within.[32] While Whitefield was traveling in Virginia, someone actually took him for a Quaker because, as he wrote, "he heard me talk of the necessity of being born again of the Spirit."[33]

From this central belief in direct inspiration both Quakers and Evangelicals derived certain corollaries: (1) the depravity of the unregenerate natural man, (2) the freedom of the will and the universality of Christ's atonement, and (3) the possibility of perfection. There were also certain practical consequences of their common emphasis on the Spirit: (1) a prophetic note in their preaching and an austere moral code, (2) a strong humanitarian impulse, (3) a disparagement of reason and theological education, and (4) a democratic tendency.

The Quakers shared with the Evangelicals a gloomy view of unregenerate human nature. Wesley's insistent dwelling upon human depravity is well known, and it was natural that Whitefield as a Calvinist should have kept this tenet in the foreground of his preaching. It is not so generally understood, however, that the Quakers, particularly in the eighteenth century, regarded the natural man as corrupt and fallen. Yet George Fox wrote that "all are concluded under sin and shut up in unbelief," and Robert Barclay devoted a long chapter in his *Apology* to a discussion of man's sinful nature.[34] Barclay's emphasis on depravity made a strong impression on the Quakerism of the eighteenth century; indeed it was, in Rufus M. Jones's view, one of the chief sources of quietism in the Society of Friends.[35]

In the second place, the emphasis on personal experience fostered in both Quakerism and Methodist Evangelicalism a tendency toward voluntarism and universalism. This statement is subject to reservations in the case of the Calvinist Whitefield and the Presbyterians of the Middle Colonies; but even of them, as of the followers of Jonathan Edwards in New England, one can say that the practical exigencies of revival preaching and the rising tide of humanitarianism made breaches in the traditional theological structure based on determinism and limited atonement. Wesley, of course, was an outright Arminian, and the tendency of the Evangelical movement everywhere was to enlarge the area of freedom for the human will, to promote the idea that Christ died for all men and not for a few only. Both of these deductions had been drawn by the primitive Friends from their principle of the Inner Light: they repudiated election and reprobation, asserting the freedom of the will, and they expressed and acted upon the conviction that the divine Seed was in *every* man.[36]

Both the early Quakers and the Methodists asserted the possibility that a man who yielded himself to the working of the divine in him might cast off the incubus of sin completely and thus become perfect while yet on the earth. This doctrine has been a stumbling block to many, and yet neither the early Friends nor the Methodists shrank from drawing this inference from their major premise.[37]

The basic emphasis on inner experience had certain practical consequences which gave a common color to the social message and testimonies of the two groups. George Fox and his coadjutors were, in the first instance, prophets of righteousness, products and promoters of the Puritan revolt, and exponents of the Puritan ideal of intramundane asceticism. Fox's primary definition of the Inner Light, as Rachel Hadley King has shown, was "that which shows a man evil,"[38] and the burden of most early Quaker preaching consisted in calling men off from the vanities and iniquities of the world. The Evangelical movement likewise, in one of its major aspects, was a rigoristic protest against the worldliness and moral laxity of Georgian England, an outcropping of that vein of moralism which is indigenous to the Anglo-Saxon character.

In their humanitarianism also the two groups shared common ground. Concern for the unfortunate has been a persistent tradition in the Society of Friends from the time of George Fox and John Bellers to that of the American Friends Service Committee. In no period was humanitarianism more prominent among Friends than in the period with which we are concerned in this essay—the period of John Woolman and Anthony Benezet. It is generally recognized that the Evangelical movement, influenced in some degree by the example of Continental Pietism, but more by its inherent emotionality, was likewise a potent contributor to the growth of modern humanitarianism. Indeed, one of the main purposes of Whitefield's travels through the American colonies was to raise funds for the Orphan House at Bethesda, Georgia, inspired by the Pietist Francke's orphan asylum in Halle.

As a consequence of their enthronement of the experiential element in religion, both Quakers and Evangelicals tended to depreciate reason as a trustworthy guide in religious matters. Barclay expressed his view in a striking simile:

As God gave two great lights to rule the outward world, the sun and the moon, the greater light to rule the day, and the lesser light to rule the night; so hath he given man the light of his Son, a spiritual divine light, to rule him in things spiritual, and the light of reason to rule him in things natural. And even as the moon borrows her light from the sun, so ought men, if they would be comfortably ordered in natural things, to have their reason enlightened by this divine and pure light.[39]

Wesley likewise inveighed against the barren rationalism of his age, and contended that reason is impotent except as it is subordinate to the spiritual senses: "Till you have these internal senses, till the eyes of your understanding are opened, you can have no proper apprehension of divine things, no just idea of them. Nor consequently can you either judge truly or reason justly concerning them; seeing your reason has no ground whereon to stand, no materials to work upon."[40] This antirationalism led both Friends and Evangelicals to set little store by formal training in theology as preparation for the ministry. This is not to say that they had no use for theology; it is merely to say that they were both concerned about the spiritual inadequacy of a "hireling clergy" or, to borrow a phrase from Gilbert Tennent, "the dangers of an unconverted ministry." Theological knowledge was regarded as a snare unless it was subservient to a regenerate spirit. It is no mere coincidence that the Quakers and the Methodists should both have developed lay preaching into an effective instrument for the propagation of their message.

The potential universality of divine inspiration implied the equality of all men in the sight of God, and this in turn had obvious democratic implications. This leveling tendency was reinforced by the fact that both Quakers and Methodists had recruited their members in the first instance largely from the lower classes. In the popular mind both groups were associated with the idea of social revolution. In the case of the Quakers this conception was fostered by the stubborn refusal to uncover the head in the presence of social superiors and the disuse of the pronoun *you* as a mark of respect in addressing an individual of higher station. The Methodists in their turn were accused of holding doctrines "strongly tinctured with impertinence and disrespect toward their superiors, in perpetually endeavoring to level all ranks and do away with all distinctions."[41]

While noting these similarities, we should not overlook the differences between Quakerism and Evangelicalism. Neither Wesley nor Whitefield ever allowed his insistence upon immediate religious experience to obscure the importance of doctrinal orthodoxy. If the principal historical result of the Evangelical Revival was to revive inward personal religion, it was hardly less important in fastening a new orthodoxy upon the English-speaking world. Basic in this orthodoxy were the traditional Protestant doctrines of the Trinity, the Deity of Christ, the Vicarious Atonement, and the plenary inspiration and authority of the Scriptures. The early Friends had been sound on all these points;[42] but they differed from the later Evangelicals in not making correct belief essential to salvation. As William Penn put it: "It is not opinion, or speculation, or notions of what is true, or assent to, or the subscription of articles or propositions, though never so soundly worded, that according to their sense makes a man a true believer, or a true Christian. But it is a conformity of mind and practice to the will of God, in all holiness of conversation, according to the dictates of this divine principle of light and life in the soul, which denotes a person truly a child of God."[43] The eighteenth century Friends tended to regard any concern with theological doctrine as "creaturely activity," and consequently to view it with profound distrust.[44] Nor did they have any sympathy with those outward ordinances of the church by which Wesley and Whitefield, as priests of the Church of England, set such store.

4

In spite of divergences at certain points, however, there remains a wide area of fundamental agreement between Quakerism and Evangelicalism. How, then, are we to account for the coolness of the Philadelphia Quakers to a movement which was in such large measure a republication of their own religion of spiritual illumination? The answer is to be found (1) by examining the conception of the nature of the Spirit's working held by the primitive Friends in common with the early Evangelical leaders, and contrasting it with the conception held by those later Friends who were contemporary with the Great Awakening; and (2) by exploring some of the social implications of these contrasting views.

Broadly speaking, the type of religious sensibility characteristic of George Fox and his compeers as well as of Whitefield and the Evangelicals was *enthusiastic* rather than *mystical*.[45] Failure to recognize this fact on the part of students who have lumped Fox with the mystics has led to a misunderstanding of his personality and the nature of the movement he founded. For the mystic the knowledge of God comes about through a process which has been described as "regenerative gradualism,"[46] a process of slow progression through successive stages of spiritual awareness to final absorption in the Absolute. "The Enthusiast . . . on the other hand, tended to conceive the knowledge of God as coming about less methodically, as striking him with a transforming power that worked without undue delay. . . . Having once been blasted with excess of light, the Enthusiast easily overcame temptations and doubts and soon established a privileged intimate relationship with God that required little further improvement, no elaboration of nuances. . . . The Enthusiast, in other words, was brought into *rapport* with God by what may be called the process of inspirational automatism in contra-distinction to the Mystic's of regenerative gradualism."[47] The enthusiast is typically a person of extremely unstable psychic equilibrium, subject to visions, voices, trances, involuntary muscular reactions, and the other sensory and motor automatisms with which the student of the psychopathology of religion is familiar.

George Fox's temperament was that of the enthusiast par excellence. With him the experience of divine inspiration was not the consequence of a long and arduous advance through successive stages of "awakening," "purgation," "illumination," and "the dark night of the soul" to ultimate union with the Godhead. The crucial experience of his life, wherein he knew "experimentally" that there was one, even Christ Jesus, that could speak to his condition,[48] came, to be sure, after a long period of "seeking" during which he had applied to many of the spiritual physicians and quacks who abounded in Commonwealth England; but when the experience of the divine presence came, it came in a blinding flash, and having come, it was never wholly to leave him, but was always with him in the form of "movings," "openings," impulses, admonitions, commands, of whose divine origin he never had the slightest doubt. The mystic's meditation and contemplation were foreign to his nature; he was a religious activist who never had to wait for spiritual leading. His "movings" and "openings" were unlike the ineffable ecstasies of the mystic in that they were definite, unequivocal revelations of new truths, prompting him to specific actions. The content of these experiences could be reduced to words, and, like the pronouncements of the Hebrew prophets, prefaced by "Thus saith the Lord." The evidence seems to indicate that the other early Quaker leaders were by and large of the enthusiastic rather than the mystical type, and that their religious experience had more in common with the wind, the earthquake, and the fire than with the still small voice.

When Whitefield appeared on the scene, his doctrine was at once recognized as a resurgence of the enthusiasm of Fox. One contemporary observer took the trouble to compile a series of roughly parallel passages from the journals of the two men, and declared that "it must . . . manifestly appear to every candid and unprejudiced Reader of these Abstracts, that George Fox, the Father of the Quakers, and the Reverend Mr. George Whitefield, one of the Apostles of the Methodists, in many Respects resemble each other; and that, notwithstanding they may possibly differ in some particular Points and Sentiments, they are both fond of the same Phrase and Diction; and their Pretences to Inspiration, to a very intimate Familiarity with the Deity, and the Power of working Miracles, are of the same Stamp and Authority." This writer did not imply that Whitefield was a conscious imitator of Fox, but contented himself with the comment that who-

compares the two journals "may, without a Spirit of Divination, pronounce them both to proceed from an enthusiastic Spirit."[49]

The mood of quietism crept over the Society of Friends in the early eighteenth century, however, and the enthusiast gave way to the mystic as the normal Quaker type. No longer was there the sudden dazzling and transforming experience and thereafter the constant presence of the Godhead, prompting to action. Instead there was more likely to be a slow and gradual development with frequent extended periods of "dryness" and occasional refreshing seasons of spiritual receptivity. Communion with God was an experience to be sought after by a process of "centering down," ceasing from "creaturely activity," and dying to self and the insistent demands of the natural man. It was not a sudden and unexpected flash of recognition as with Fox, but a gradual and progressive awareness. John Woolman writes: "As I lived under the cross and simply followed the openings of truth, my mind from day to day was more enlightened."[50] Whereas Fox had always known his "openings" and "movings" to be of divine origin, the eighteenth century Quaker was cautious lest they be from the devil or from man's carnal nature. The change can be summed up by saying that the religious sensibility of the eighteenth century Quaker was predominantly mystical rather than enthusiastic.

This shift having taken place, it is not strange that the staid and placid Philadelphia Friends should have been shocked and perhaps embarrassed by the reenactment in the quiet streets of Philadelphia of scenes like those which they had so recently put behind them. Having passed beyond religious emotionalism into peaceful introspection, they found it painful, one may infer, to be reminded by the antics of the revivalists that they, too, had once been violent extroverts and fanatics whose behavior had been indecorous in the extreme. In their new-found respectability and sophistication they preferred to dissociate themselves completely from a movement that recalled too vividly their own origins.[51]

Closely allied to this may have been a revulsion from the lower-class character of the revival and from the suspicion of social radicalism which attached to it. One may conjecture that, having risen within a few generations from a lower-class to an upper-middle-class position in society, the Quaker merchants had no desire to be associated in anyone's mind with a religious movement which was making headway in the same social class from which they themselves had originated in the previous century. If they had anything in common with other social parvenus, they undoubtedly wanted to forget, and to cause others to forget, that they had sprung out of the *mobile vulgus*. The Great Awakening was all too obviously reminiscent of their own social origins.

Enthusiasm had long been associated in the minds of many with the revolutionary social and political movements of the Commonwealth period. Any democratic doctrine was likely in the eighteenth century to be branded as both leveling and enthusiastic, not only by Tories but also by Whig moderates who desired social quiet in order to preserve the stable equilibrium established by the Glorious Revolution of 1688. Insofar as they had any political sympathies, the great Quaker merchants tended at this period to be Whiggish, and they were as fearful of revolutionary social movements as any other propertied class.

Here on the streets of Philadelphia two of the most characteristic religious movements in Anglo-Saxon Protestantism in a sense confronted each other. Theologically they were at one in many essential respects. In 1740, however, they were in different stages in their historical development. The Evangelical movement, then in its robust and dynamic infancy, was characterized by that type of powerful religious sensibility known as enthusiasm, and drew its strength chiefly from the lower classes. Quakerism, on the other hand, was well advanced in that historical development to which such religious movements appear to be inevitably subject:[52] it had passed from uninhibited enthusiasm to quietistic mysticism, and what had once been a plebeian movement had become in Philadelphia the religion of a substantial mercantile aristocracy. In the psychological attitude produced by the juxtaposition of the two groups may be found the reason why in the midst of the heated currents of religious enthusiasm "The Quaker kept the way of his own,/A non-conductor among the wires,/ With coat of asbestos proof to fires."

CHAPTER VII

The Culture of Early Pennsylvania

In Pennsylvania after 1682 the Friends had an opportunity to create a self-contained culture. William Penn's province was a British colony, but it was also designed to be a "colony of heaven," an extended Quaker meeting making its corporate witness to the Truth, a society of people responsive to the Inward Light and living under a government whose fundamental law was the Sermon on the Mount. Penn himself referred to it as a "holy experiment," and he clearly expected that in Pennsylvania religion and culture would be synonymous and that his colonists would be led into a way of life so consistent with the Truth inwardly revealed that no conflict of values, much less of arms, could arise.

The experiment did not turn out precisely as Penn had planned. As we have seen, the early Pennsylvanians did contrive to translate their religious testimonies for peace, equality, simplicity, and community into social and political facts to a remarkable degree. But imperceptibly the relative values of the "world" crept in, while the perfectionist testimonies tended to congeal into dogmas increasingly irrelevant to the facts of American life. In the end, the Quakers chose to salvage their religious values by seceding, as it were, from the world politically and to some extent socially. According to Daniel J. Boorstin, the failure of the Friends to adapt their values to the realities of American experience was "one of the greatest lost opportunities in all American history." Two flaws, he thinks, were "fatal to the influence of this remarkable people on American culture . . . first . . . a preoccupation with the purity of their own souls; and, second, a rigidity in all their beliefs."[1]

Perhaps so. Or perhaps the "failure" of the Pennsylvania Quakers, if it was a failure, illustrated an inevitable tension between Christ

114

and culture, between the demands of the Inward Light and the claims of civilization. If that tension is to be creatively maintained within history, if human culture is not to become a law unto itself, indifferent to the imperatives of a higher law, it is essential that some individuals and groups should bear witness, however imperfectly, to the Truth beyond culture. Perhaps this was the historic role of the Quakers in the Atlantic civilization.

But, not to end this book on too theological a note—for theology is neither the genius of Quakerism nor the specialty of this author— there is another significance to the story of Quakerism and culture which is illustrated by the history of early Pennsylvania. William Penn, true to the Quaker insistence on "that of God in every man," opened the doors of his province to all men, especially to the religious dissenters and the economically oppressed, the harried, persecuted, and miserable of the Atlantic world. They accepted his invitation and swarmed across the sea, especially from the continent of Europe, thus broadening the scope of the Atlantic Community. The people of Pennsylvania, Penn could write as early as 1685, "are a collection of divers nations in Europe, as French, Dutch, Germans, Swedes, Danes, Finns, Scotch, Irish, and English."[2] Each group brought its own culture to Pennsylvania, and each group, once settled there, began the process of cultural borrowing and lending which ultimately produced a new amalgam to enrich the Atlantic civilization. To have provided a setting for that great experiment was in itself a notable Quaker contribution to modern culture.

1

Benjamin West has a lot to answer for. Everyone knows his painting of William Penn's treaty with the Indians; it is one of our national icons, "as indelibly impressed on the American mind," it has been said, "as . . . Washington's crossing of the Delaware."[3] The lush greens of its foliage, the tawny flesh tones of its noble savages, the sober drab of its Quaker plain dress have fixed forever in our consciousness a stereotype of early Pennsylvania. There he stands under the great elm at Shackamaxon, portly and benignant, the Founder of the Quaker commonwealth, eternally dispensing peace and yard goods to the Indians. If it is mostly legend—for there is no documentary record of a treaty at Shackamaxon—it is at least an inspiring one, quite as much so as that of Pocahontas laying her lovely head on Captain John Smith's breast or Squanto instructing the Pilgrim Fathers in the mysteries of maize culture. And whatever its faults as a document or as a painting, it has the merit of a certain truth to history, for, unlike the founders of Jamestown and Plymouth, the Quaker founders of Pennsylvania did contrive by fair dealing and generosity to stay at peace with the local Indians for three-quarters of a century.

What is wrong, then, with West's vast, idyllic canvas as a symbol of early Pennsylvania? It is not the anachronisms that bother me. True, the architectural background is composed of brick buildings that could not have been standing in 1682; true, West portrays Penn as stout and middle-aged when in fact he was still young and athletic, and dressed him in the Quaker Oats costume of shadbelly coat and cocked hat that Friends did not wear for half a century to come. No, the mischief lies in the aura, the atmosphere, of the painting—the air of smug and stupid piety combined with the stolid respectability of the successful bourgeois. No one will deny that the early Quakers were a "God-fearing, money-making people"—least of all I, who have written a book on the proposition that they had one foot in the meetinghouse and the other in the countinghouse. It is probably unfair to demand of a painter that he project the life of the mind on his canvas; perhaps it takes a modern abstractionist to portray a pure idea. Yet I cannot help regretting that the most widely current stereotype of early Pennsylvania should suggest a cultural and intellectual desert.

Besides, early Pennsylvania was not, of course, just Quaker. Everyone who has seen *Plain and Fancy* knows about the Amish, who have been here for a long time, and everyone who has a taste for the quaint and the indigestible knows about "hex signs" on barns (which have nothing to do, of course, with witches) and shoofly pie. If we don't know about the Scotch-Irish, it is not for want of zeal on the part of their descendants, who would have us believe that they fought the Indians and won the American Revolution all by themselves. And anyone who has traversed Philadelphia's "Main Line" has the vague impression that that region was once peopled by Welshmen, who left the landscape strewn with odd-sounding place names like Llanerch, Bala-Cynwyd, and Tredyffrin (actually, most of those names were chosen from a gazetteer by a nineteenth century president of the Pennsylvania Railroad looking for distinctive names for his suburban stations).

What I want to suggest is that early Pennsylvania had a genuine and important culture or complex of cultures, that there was something more to it than simple Quaker piety and commercialism on the one hand and ethnic quaintness on the other. I am going to sidestep one basic problem by refusing to define exactly what I mean by "culture." The anthropologically minded will be annoyed by my irresponsible tendency to use the term now as Ruth Benedict would use it and again perhaps as Matthew Arnold would use it. In justification of this slipshod procedure I can only plead that I am merely an unscientific historian, not a "social scientist."[4]

"Early Pennsylvania" I will define more strictly. By this term I shall mean Pennsylvania east of the Susquehanna and south of the Blue Mountains in the period down to about 1740. But I must immediately point out that this area was never a self-contained or self-conscious regional unit. It was part of a larger geographical whole. The men in gray flannel suits have been trying hard in recent years to impress upon us the concept "Delaware Valley, U.S.A." The colonial Pennsylvanian knew without being told that he lived in the valley of the Delaware. He first saw his new home from the deck of a ship sailing up the great river. His prosperity and his comfort depended in large measure on the commerce that carried his farm products down the river to the West Indies and southern Europe, that brought back up the river the textiles and hardware he needed and could not manufacture for himself. The Delaware united West Jersey, Pennsylvania, and the Lower Counties (which eventually became the state of Delaware) into a single economic province, and linked it with the rest of the Atlantic Community. It also unified the valley into a single "culture area." The Quakers' Yearly Meeting embraced Friends on both sides of the river, and met alternately at Philadelphia on the west bank and Burlington on the east. The Anglicans also thought of the valley as a unit, a single missionary field to be saved from "Quakerism or heathenism." I shall restrict myself, however, to that portion of it which originally formed the province of Pennsylvania proper—the counties of Bucks, Philadelphia, and Chester.

2

The Founder of Pennsylvania, we must be clear, was neither a narrow-minded religious zealot on the one hand nor a mean-spirited Philistine on the other. William Penn was a man of broad intellectual culture in Matthew Arnold's sense, educated at Oxford, on the Continent, and at Lincoln's Inn; he was a Fellow of the Royal Society and the associate not only of kings and courtiers, but of the reigning intellectuals of the day—men like Samuel Pepys, the diarist; John Locke, the philosopher; Sir William Petty, the political economist. He was a man of wide reading. The list of books he bought to bring to America on his second visit suggests his range; it included the poems of Milton, a copy of *Don Quixote*, the works of John Locke, the latest travel books by William Dampier and Father Hennepin, the Roman histories of Livy and Suetonius.[5] Penn was a good Quaker and a shrewd real-estate promoter, but he was also—though one would scarcely guess it from Benjamin West's canvas—a Restoration egghead, as much at home with the philosophers of the Royal Society as with the Indians of the Pennsylvania forest. The example of such a man was enough to ensure that Pennsylvania would not be a cultural desert. And Penn's commitment to a sophisticated ideal of religious freedom meant that the intellectual life of his colony would never stagnate for want of controversy and the creative clash of opinions.

It is true that, by and large, the English Quakers who sailed with Penn on the *Welcome* or followed him on other ships did not come, as he did, from the leisure class. Quakerism in the seventeenth century took root in the lower orders of society, among the yeoman farmers, husbandmen, artisans, shopkeepers, hired servants, men and women who worked with their hands. The farmers among them, poverty-stricken dalesmen from the moors of northern England, headed straight for the rich uplands of Bucks and Chester counties. (As late as the middle of the eighteenth century, the people of Chester still spoke in a broad Yorkshire dialect.[6]) Within a few years they were producing flour and meat for export. With the proceeds they built those neat stone farmhouses with their projecting pent roofs and door hoods that are so charming when one comes upon them in the midst of the split-levels and ranch houses of Philadelphia's exurbia.

They had little beyond the rudiments of reading and writing, these rural Friends, and few books beyond the Bible and Barclay's *Apology*. They had little time for reading; besides, their Quakerism enjoined upon them a sober, plain way of life. But if their lives seem drab, remember the clean lines, the satisfying proportions, the functional perfection of the stone meetinghouse where they gathered on First Day to worship God in the living silence. In that simple structure form followed function with a faithfulness that Frank Lloyd Wright might have envied, and every superfluity was stripped away to leave its purpose revealed in utter purity. The Pennsylvania Friends even anticipated a favorite device of the modern architect: they installed sliding panels with which they could break up the "flow of space" and convert their oblong meetinghouses into two rooms for the men's and women's meetings for business.

Howard Brinton calls the period from 1700 to 1740 the Golden Age of Quakerism in America. He is thinking primarily of the rural Quakers of Bucks and Chester counties when he describes, with a touch of nostalgia, the "unique Quaker culture" of the period:

In the Quaker communities the meeting was the center, spiritually, intellectually and economically. It included a library and a school. Disputes of whatever nature were settled in the business sessions of the meeting. The poor were looked after, moral delinquents dealt with, marriages approved and performed. . . . Each group, centered in the meeting, was a well-ordered, highly integrated community of interdependent members. . . . This flowering of Quakerism was not characterized by any outburst of literary or artistic production. Its whole emphasis was on life itself in home, meeting and community. This life was an artistic creation as beautiful in its simplicity and proportion as was the architecture of its meeting houses. The "Flowering of New England" has been described in terms of its literature, but the flowering of Quakerism in the middle colonies can be described only in terms of life itself.[7]

Quaker life in Philadelphia soon fell into a different pattern. Eventually the cleavage between rural and urban Quaker culture would split the Society of Friends into two factions, Hicksite and Orthodox (and one might even suggest that the recent healing of the schism was made easier by the blurring of that sharp line of cleavage

in our twentieth century suburban culture). The material basis for
the rise of urban Quaker culture was Philadelphia's amazing growth
and prosperity. Last of the major colonial cities to be founded, William Penn's "green country town" quickly outstripped New York,
Newport, and Charleston, and by 1740 was pressing the much older
town of Boston hard for primacy in wealth and population.[8]

By 1740 the Quakers were already a minority group in the Quaker
City, but they had been the prime movers in the town's economic
expansion and they still controlled a large share of its trade and its
visible assets. Most of the early immigrants had been craftsmen and
shopkeepers. They practiced the economic ethic of Poor Richard long
before Benjamin Franklin, that Johnny-come-lately, arrived in Philadelphia. Working diligently in their callings, they quickly transformed
a primitive frontier village into a complex provincial market town and
business center. The tons of wheat and flour, the barrels of beef and
pork, the lumber, the bales of furs that poured into Philadelphia
from the hinterland provided, of course, the substance of Philadelphia's flourishing export trade. But it was the diligence and business
acumen of the Quaker merchants that translated those raw goods
into prosperity for the whole region.

But prosperity, it must be admitted, had its effects on Philadelphia
Quakerism. As wealth increased, plainness in "dress and address"
declined, as we noted earlier. As early as 1695 Philadelphia Yearly
Meeting was warning its male members against wearing "long lapp'd
Sleeves or Coates gathered at the Sides, or Superfluous Buttons, or
Broad Ribbons about their Hatts, or long curled Perriwiggs," and
cautioning women Friends against "Dressing their Heads Immod-
estly, or Wearing their Garments undecently . . . or Wearing . . .
Striped or Flower'd Stuffs, or other useless and Superfluous Things."[9]
Obviously, the Yearly Meeting wouldn't have bothered to discourage
its members from wearing these abominations unless some Friends
were actually doing so. But the clever Quaker, as we have seen, could
find ways to outwit the meeting, could practice conspicuous consumption without violating the letter of the discipline.[10] In other words,
the Philadelphia Friends were becoming worldly, and there were
Jeremiahs—especially among the country Friends—who insisted that
vital Quakerism varied inversely with the prosperity of its adherents.[11]

I am not concerned at the moment with moral judgments. I am

concerned with "culture," loosely defined, and I must therefore point out that the Quaker aristocrats of Philadelphia were receptive not only to the fashions of the "world's people," but to their architecture, their books, their ideas as well, though there was always something sober and substantial about Quaker houses, libraries, and intellectual pursuits, as there was about Quaker clothes. If rural Pennsylvania Quakerism flowered in ordered and beautiful lives, the Quakerism of Philadelphia flowered in many realms of the mind and spirit, particularly in the fields of organized humanitarianism, science, and medicine. Since they had no use for a learned clergy, the Quakers were slow to establish colleges, but the humane and learned institutions which gave Philadelphia its cultural preeminence in the pre-Revolutionary years—the American Philosophical Society, the Library Company, the Pennsylvania Hospital, even the College of Philadelphia, which became the University of Pennsylvania—all owed more than a little to the solid and generous culture of the Quaker merchants.[12]

If I limit myself to mentioning the cultural interests and achievements of just one Philadelphia Quaker—James Logan—it is because he is the one I know best. I shall not contend that Logan was either a typical Philadelphian or a representative Friend. The breadth and reach of his mind would have made him an exceptional man in any time or place; and as for his Quakerism, he sat so loose to it that Philadelphia Monthly Meeting had to deal with him repeatedly for breaches of the discipline. But a résumé of James Logan's contributions in the realm of "high culture" should lay to rest any lingering suspicions that early Philadelphia was a Sahara of the intellect.

Logan came to Philadelphia in 1699 as William Penn's secretary. At one time or another over the next half-century he occupied nearly every responsible public office in the province, including those of chief justice and acting governor. He was Pennsylvania's leading fur merchant, her ablest and most respected Indian diplomat. He was the builder of Philadelphia's most distinguished early Georgian mansion—the house called Stenton, which still stands in its elegant Quaker simplicity amid the ugliness of industrial North Philadelphia. He assembled a library of three thousand volumes which I do not hesitate to call the best-chosen collection of books in all colonial America. Unlike most other colonial libraries, it is still intact at the

Library Company of Philadelphia. And unlike many other colonial libraries, it was a scholar's working library. Logan's marginal annotations make it clear how closely he studied his learned books in many tongues. He carried on a correspondence in Latin—the universal language of scholarship—with Dr. Johann Albertus Fabricius of Hamburg, the most erudite classicist of his age, and his commentaries on Euclid and Ptolemy were published in Hamburg and Amsterdam. He made a translation of Cicero's essay on old age which Benjamin Franklin, its publisher, hailed as "a happy omen that Philadelphia shall become the seat of the American Muses." He designed and carried out some experiments on the generation of Indian corn that botanists all over Europe cited for a century or more as proof that sex reared its head in the plant kingdom. He was certainly one of the first Americans to understand and use Sir Isaac Newton's method of fluxions, or calculus. He made contributions to the science of optics, which were published in Holland, and several of his scientific papers were read before the Royal Society of London and printed in its *Philosophical Transactions*. He crowned his intellectual life by writing a treatise on moral philosophy which, unfortunately, was never finished and never published. That treatise, which exists only in fragments, may have been suggested by an offhand remark of the great John Locke that it should be possible to construct a rational science of morals: Logan called it in typical eighteenth century fashion, "The Duties of Man Deduced from Nature."[13]

James Logan, I repeat, was not a typical Philadelphia Quaker, but the example of such a man—and remember, he was the leading public figure of his day—could not fail to stimulate others to the intellectual life. Indeed, the three men who are usually called Philadelphia's first scientists—Benjamin Franklin, John Bartram, the botanist, and Thomas Godfrey, the inventor of the mariners' quadrant—all owed a great deal to Logan's encouragement and patronage.

Here then, were two conflicting, or at least divergent, Quaker cultures in early Pennsylvania. A third—perhaps we should call it a subculture—flourished transiently in the frontier region, west of the Schuylkill, known as the "Welsh Tract." It is difficult to form an accurate picture of the early Welsh community. There are massive works on the subject, but they are all heavily genealogical in emphasis, and read more like stud books than like works of history: they seem more concerned with providing a suitable ancestry for later generations of Philadelphians than with disclosing the actual outlines of life in the Welsh Tract.

Were the settlers of Merion, Haverford, and Radnor rich or poor? We get no clear answer because the truth is obscured by a conflict of myths. On the one hand, to fit the legend of America as a land of opportunity, a haven for the oppressed, they must be poor men, fleeing from persecution. On the other hand, to satisfy our itch for highborn ancestors, they must be aristocrats, country squires, gentlemen to the manner born.[14] The size of some of the early landholdings and the inventories of some personal estates suggest that a few wealthy Welshmen did take up their residence on the Main Line in the 1680's and 1690's. But alongside the purchasers of two and three thousand acres who signed themselves "gentleman" were scores of yeomen, grocers, tailors, and the like, who settled on one hundred or one hundred fifty acres. The bulk of the Welsh immigrants were probably of "the middling sort" of people who gave the North American colonies and eventually the United States their overwhelming middle-class character.

Neither poverty nor persecution really explains that emigration from Wales which began as soon as William Penn opened the doors of Pennsylvania and lasted till some Quaker communities in Wales were all but depopulated. Professor A. H. Dodd, a learned student of Welsh history, has pointed out that if poverty had been at the root of this folk movement, it would have stemmed from the economically backward regions of Anglesey and Caernarvon rather than from fertile and prosperous Merionethshire, Radnorshire, and Montgomeryshire. And had persecution been the main impetus, the stream of emigration would have slacked off with the coming of toleration in 1689, instead of continuing, as it did, into the next century.[15]

If we would identify the fundamental "cause" of the Welsh migration, we must recognize that it was not the "pushing" factors of poverty or persecution at home, but the strong "pulling" force of a dream —the powerful but delusive dream of a new Wales in the western wilderness, in which, as the Welsh immigrants put it themselves, "we might live together as a civil society to endeavor to decide all controversies and debates amongst ourselves in a Gospel order, and not to entangle ourselves with laws in an unknown tongue."[16] So the first

Welsh settlers extracted from William Penn a verbal promise that they should have a 40,000-acre enclave west of the Schuylkill where they could speak their own language, practice their own customs, and hold their own courts in splendid isolation.

Their attempt to transplant their ancient culture and preserve it intact did not prosper. Within a few decades they had lost their identity and merged with the fast-growing American society around them. They blamed William Penn for the failure of their dream. It was true that his governor, confronted with a solid Welsh voting bloc, followed the time-honored principle of divide and rule: he split the Welsh Tract in two by running a county line through the middle of it, throwing Haverford and Radnor into Chester County, leaving only Merion in Philadelphia County. But the experiment, one suspects, was doomed from the start. The Welsh, after all, were a bilingual people, as fluent in English as in their own tongue, and there is little evidence that distinctive Welsh laws or customs were observed in the Tract. It was not long before David ap Rees became David Price, Ellis ap Hugh became Ellis Pugh, and Edward ap John became plain Edward Jones.

It is not clear how long even such national traits as the love of music persisted. Thomas Allen Glenn found it pleasant "to think that often through the wild woodland of Colonial Merion there has echoed the burthen of some ancient British war song, chanted ages ago in battle against the legions of Imperial Rome." But Charles H. Browning, who compiled the fullest account of Welsh life in Pennsylvania, could not find "even a tradition that the Welsh Friends over the Schuylkill were inclined to music, singing and dancing." There is a revealing story about Edward Foulke, one of the pioneer settlers of Gwynedd. While he was still in Wales and not yet joined with the Quakers, people used to collect on Sundays at his house at Coed-y-foel in Merionethshire to join him in song, for Edward was a fine singer. But he and his wife presently became uneasy in their minds about this idle way of spending the Lord's Day. Thereafter, when his musical friends gathered and he was tempted to "undue levity," he would get out the Bible and read it aloud. It was surprising, says an old account, how quickly "the light and unprofitable portion of his visitors" melted away.[17] When Edward Foulke came to the Quaker settlement of Gwynedd in 1698, it is safe to assume that he left his harp behind. The war songs of the ancient Britons may have rung out in the Merion woods, but the echo that Thomas Allen Glenn thought he caught over the centuries was more likely the sound of the psalms of David sung in the Baptist chapels of the Welsh Tract. In any case there is little reason to think that the Welsh Friends after a few decades in America differed much from their English coreligionists.

The original settlers of Germantown seem to have suffered a like fate. The late Professor William I. Hull was convinced that they were predominantly Dutch, not German, in culture, and Quaker, not Mennonite, in religion.[18] But whatever their origins, they quickly became Philadelphia Friends, like the Welsh. Their very names they Anglicized from Luykens to Lukens, from Kunders to Conard, from Schumacher to Shoemaker. Those Dutchmen who were not assimilated to Anglo-Saxon Quakerism were presently swallowed up by the great tide of Swiss and Germans who came to Pennsylvania after 1709—the people who, to add to the general confusion, are known as the "Pennsylvania Dutch."

3

I cannot here attempt a definition or characterization of Pennsylvania Dutch culture. All I can do is make a few observations about it and suggest two excellent books on the subject—Fredric Klees's *The Pennsylvania Dutch*[19] and the symposium called *The Pennsylvania Germans,* edited by Ralph Wood.[20] In the first place, Pennsylvania Dutch culture was never a single entity, a uniform way of life. Though we tend to think of it as a unity, it was and is a congeries of cultures with roots in many different geographical areas and religious traditions. Among the immigrants from continental Europe who came to Pennsylvania in a trickle during the first twenty-five years and in a flood thereafter were Alsatians and Württembergers and Swiss, a scattering of French Huguenots who had lived temporarily in the Rhine Valley, and, ultimately, some Bohemians, Silesians, and Moravians, who came to America by way of Saxony. In religious terms they fell into three broad categories: the sects or plain people, the church people, and the Moravians. All of them were pushed out of central Europe by religious persecution and economic hardship; all were pulled toward Penn's colony by the promise of religious freedom and economic opportunity. It is the sects—the Mennonites, the Amish, the Dunkers, the Schwenkfelders, the Protestant monks and nuns of Ephrata, the mystical Society of the Woman in the Wilderness— who have attracted most attention because of their peculiarities. But it was the church people—the Lutherans and the Reformed—who predominated, and it was they who established the characteristic Pennsylvania Dutch way of life. When Count Zinzendorf, the leader of the Moravians, came to Pennsylvania with a noble ecumenical dream of uniting all the German religious groups, he soon discovered how stubborn these theological and cultural differences were.

What these people had in common was chiefly that they spoke a different, a "foreign," tongue. They were, said a supercilious Philadelphian, "so profoundly ignorant as to be unable to speak the English language." Hence arose the familiar stereotype, the notion that they were boors, stupid, stolid clods—in a word, "the dumb Dutch."[21] Yet they were beyond all comparison the best farmers in colonial America. From the beginning their great barns, their neat farmyards, their care in fencing their livestock, their systematic rotation of crops, their infallible instinct for fertile limestone soil, their industry and good management drew favorable comment in a land notorious for wasteful and slovenly farming. "It is pretty to behold our back settlements," wrote Lewis Evans in 1753, "where the barns are large as palaces, while the owners live in log huts; a sign, though, of thriving farmers."[22] Evans's reference to the log cabin is a reminder that we owe that symbol of the American frontier to the Germans and to the Swedes, who had settled earlier along the Delaware River. It was no invention of the American pioneer, but a cultural importation from the forest lands of central and northern Europe.[23] As a matter of fact, we are indebted to the Pennsylvania Dutch for the two other major symbols of the frontier—the Conestoga wagon, and the so-called Kentucky rifle.[24] And consider their rich and various folk art. Beside the gay and colorful designs of tulips and hearts, distelfinks and peacocks with which they covered their dower chests and pottery and baptismal certificates, most of what passes for early American folk art seems pale and anemic. Finally, be it remembered that the plain people of the Pennsylvania Dutch country have maintained a vital and satisfying religious life longer than almost any other group in

America. Even today the simple piety of a Mennonite farmer is a real and impressive thing in the midst of much false and superficial religiosity.

Theirs was a peasant culture, and it has kept its peasant character for two centuries in a country where peasantry has always been alien. Professor Robert Redfield's generic description of peasant values describes their outlook fairly accurately: "an intense attachment to native soil; a reverent disposition toward habitat and ancestral ways; a restraint on individual self-seeking in favor of family and community; a certain suspiciousness, mixed with appreciation, of town life; a sober and earthy ethic."[25] Unquestionably, early Pennsylvania Dutch life was limited, lacking in intellectual quality, wanting in many of the higher values of civilized life. And yet, having said that, one immediately asks: where in early America except in the Moravian towns of Bethlehem and Nazareth and Lititz could one hear Bach and Handel, Haydn and Mozart, performed by full orchestra and chorus?

The tide of German immigration set toward the full around 1710 and reached the flood at mid-century. Hardly had the old settlers begun to adjust to these newcomers with their strange tongue and stranger ways before they became aware of a new inundation of land-hungry immigrants—the people who have always been known in America as the Scotch-Irish—Scottish and Presbyterian in culture, Irish only in that they had been living for a longer or shorter period in Ulster. They came in waves, the first after 1717, the second about ten years later, the third around the year 1740. Their coming in such crowds and their free-and-easy attitude toward details like land titles took even James Logan aback, although he was a Scotch-Irishman himself. They simply squatted, he complained, wherever they found "a spot of vacant ground." When challenged to show title, he added, a little sadly, their standard response was that it was "against the laws of God and nature that so much land should lie idle while so many Christians wanted it to labor on and raise their bread."[26]

It was actually James Logan who assigned them their historic role in America. It happened that the Indians across the Susquehanna were growing restive just as the first wave of Scotch-Irish settlers was reaching Philadelphia. Though Logan was a Quaker, he did not share

William Penn's faith in pacifism. Recalling from his own childhood
how gallantly the Protestants of Ulster had defended Londonderry
and Inniskillen against the Roman Catholic forces of James II, he
"thought it might be prudent" to plant a settlement of these tough,
bellicose Ulstermen on the Susquehanna "as a *frontier* in case of any
disturbance."[27] Logan used the term "frontier" with a specific, limited
meaning; he meant a border garrison, a strong point on the edge of
hostile territory. But the word was destined to vibrate with special
overtones for Americans as the outer edge of settlement crept across
the continent. And on nearly every American frontier, the Scotch-
Irish—those doughty, Bible-quoting, whisky-drinking, gun-toting,
Indian-fighting Presbyterians whom James Logan planted in his garrison town of Donegal on the Susquehanna—would be the defenders
of the marches, the tamers of the wilderness, the advance agents of
the white man's civilization.

They were not crude, uncultivated roughnecks, these Scotch-Irish
frontiersmen. They were pious Presbyterians, and they insisted on a
learned ministry and a literate congregation. "The schoolhouse and
the kirk went together," says Carl Wittke, "wherever the Scotch-
Irish frontier moved."[28] "These fortresses against ignorance and the
devil," adds Louis B. Wright, "paralleled a chain of blockhouses and
forts against the French and Indian. The Scots were as eager to fight
one as the other."[29] New Englanders have a habit of attributing the
spread of popular education over the country to the heirs of the
Yankee Puritan. But some of the credit rightfully belongs to the
Scotch-Irish Presbyterian, who kept the lamp of learning lighted on
many an American frontier. As early as 1726 the Reverend William
Tennent established a "Log College" on Neshaminy Creek in Bucks
County, and the "Log College" was the seed out of which Princeton
University grew.

A cultural map of the settled portion of Pennsylvania in 1740
would show a band of Quaker country roughly parallel with the Delaware River and extending back twenty-five or thirty miles, its western outposts near Coatesville, Pottstown, and Quakertown. Behind it
would be a broad belt of Pennsylvania Dutch country, anchored at
Bethlehem to the northeast and at Lancaster to the southwest. Still
farther west in the Susquehanna Valley would be a sparse strip of
Scotch-Irish settlement, overlapping on its eastern side with the

Pennsylvania Dutch country and swinging eastward in upper Bucks County, near where Neshaminy Creek joins the Delaware. There were a hundred thousand people in all, perhaps more.[30] Scattered over these broad culture areas would be small pockets of people with different backgrounds—English and Welsh Baptists in the Quaker country, a handful of Roman Catholic and Jewish families in Philadelphia, four or five thousand Negroes, slaves and freedmen, and, here and there, some remnants of the ancient inhabitants of Pennsylvania—the Lenni Lenape or Delaware Indians.

Two of these "pocket groups" demand special mention. Along the Delaware south of Philadelphia lived several hundred descendants of the "old colonists"—the Swedes, Finns, and Dutch who had brought the white man's culture to the Delaware Valley long before William Penn. By the end of a century, however, they had lost most of their distinguishing characteristics and had merged with the English culture around them. In Philadelphia there was a strong and growing Anglican community, which worshiped in style in the Palladian elegance of Christ Church. Already some of the leading Quaker families had moved so far from their plainer country brethren that they began to drift over to the more fashionable Church of England. The cultural traditions of early Pennsylvania, it is clear, were in constant flux, forever forming new combinations, new patterns, in the prevailing atmosphere of social freedom and economic plenty. The variety and interrelations of these traditions give early Pennsylvania culture its peculiar significance in the development of American life.

4

It was this region primarily that Hector St. John de Crèvecœur had in mind when he asked his famous question, "What then is the American, this new man?" and sketched out the answer which has done duty for most of us ever since. The American, said Crèvecœur, is the product of a "promiscuous breed" of "English, Scotch, Irish, French, Dutch, Germans, and Swedes." Settling in the New World, he leaves behind him "all his ancient prejudices and manners [and] receives new ones from the new mode of life he has embraced, the new government he obeys, and the new rank he holds." Here, says Crèvecœur, "individuals of all nations are melted into a new race of

men, whose labors and posterity will one day cause great changes in
the world."[31] The prophecy in Crèvecœur's last words has unquestionably come true, but his account of the process by which his
American, "this new man," was created is too simple.

The familiar image of the melting pot seems to imply "a giant
caldron in which foreigners are boiled down into a colorless mass—as
insipid as any stew."[32] Clearly that is not an accurate image of early
Pennsylvania. To be sure, some groups melted. The Welsh apparently did. So did the Dutch in Germantown and the Swedes along
the Delaware. But the Germans, by and large, did not. Indeed they
seem to have become self-consciously German for the first time in
Pennsylvania: "the impact of American life," says Caroline Ware,
"tends to accentuate rather than to obliterate group consciousness"
among immigrants.[33] Some Philadelphia Quakers became Episco-
palians, but the great majority did not; and there was never any
rapprochement between the Quakers of the east and the Scotch-Irish
Presbyterians of the west. Indeed, the political history of colonial
Pennsylvania is a story of continuous struggle, not primarily between social classes or economic groups, but among cultural and religious blocs. Not assimilation but what might be called "selective
interaction" was the rule. It seems likely, for example, that the plain
dress and the plain architecture of the Amish—or at least some elements thereof—were not brought to America by the immigrants, but
were borrowed, once they had arrived, from the broadbrim hat, the
plain bonnet, and plain meetinghouse of the Quakers. By way of
return, the Pennsylvania Dutchman put scrapple and sticky cinna-
mon buns on Quaker City breakfast tables. It has even been suggested that we owe apple pie to the Pennsylvania Dutch, though as a
New Englander I shall require further evidence before I can accept
that revolutionary thesis.[34] In any case, this process of selective borrowing seems to be how American civilization was created, and there
is no better laboratory in which to observe it at work than early
Pennsylvania.

My final observation takes me from the popular culture of bonnets
and scrapple back to the level of "high culture." It is fairly well
known that from about 1740 to the end of the eighteenth century
Philadelphia was the intellectual and cultural capital of North
America. In science, in medicine, in humanitarianism, in music and

the drama and *belles lettres* its preeminence was unquestioned. How shall we explain this remarkably quick maturing in the youngest of the colonial towns? Not simply, I submit, on the ground that it was the largest and most prosperous city in the American colonies. I for one have never been convinced that high culture is a function of a high rate of income. Nor can we attribute it *all* to that displaced Bostonian, Benjamin Franklin. No, I think we shall find the source of colonial Philadelphia's flowering in the richness, the variety, and above all, in the creative interaction of the elements in its cultural hinterland.

There is nothing in Benjamin West's idyllic painting of Penn and the Indians that foreshadows the Philadelphia of Franklin and Rittenhouse, of Benjamin Rush and Charles Brockden Brown, of the American Philosophical Society and the Pennsylvania Hospital and the College of Philadelphia. But William Penn, it should be clear by now, was more than a benign dispenser of peace and yard goods to the Indians. By opening the doors of Pennsylvania to people of every nation and every religion he established a situation of cultural pluralism, and thereby created the conditions for cultural growth. And the atmosphere was freedom.

Afterword

Freedom was of the essence of the Quaker way of life as it developed within the matrix of the Atlantic culture. It was both condition and consequence. If men were to seek and follow the leadings of the Inward Light, they must be free from outward coercion by church or state, free from the mental strait-jacket of creed, from the imposed necessity of conforming to a prescribed ritual. And if they once opened themselves fully to the inshinings of the Light, they would find themselves heirs of the promise: "Ye shall know the Truth, and the Truth shall make you free." So wherever the Friends lived or traveled throughout the broad Atlantic world of the seventeenth and eighteenth centuries they sought to create and maintain an atmosphere of outward freedom not only for themselves but for all men. And in their own innermost lives they sought to abide in that freedom wherein the Inward Christ had made them free.

In both old and New England they insisted—sometimes with their lives—upon freedom of conscience. The achievement of religious toleration in England in 1689 owed something to the cogent writings of Friends like William Penn (for whom the Englishman's birthright was worth no more than a mess of pottage if it did not include "the free and uninterrupted exercise of our conscience in that way of worship we are most clearly persuaded God requires us to serve Him in"). It owed even more to the example of thousands of faithful Friends who, in the time of Charles II, suffered pain and bondage even unto death rather than give over their right to look within for the Truth. In Pennsylvania in 1682 William Penn founded his "Holy Experiment" upon the principle that the religious conscience must be utterly free. Moreover, the "Frame of Government" in which he embodied the design of that notable experiment in politics safeguarded the personal and political liberties of the freemen to a degree hardly approached anywhere else in the world of his time. And on both sides of the Atlantic Friends were in the forefront of the humanitarian crusade for the freedom of the Negro slave.

The basic freedoms which the Atlantic Community cherishes to-day—the freedoms summed up in the Atlantic Charter—are the products of many influences and long years of historical development. But in tracing their origins we cannot overlook the contribution of the Quakers.

Yet liberation from outward coercion and bondage did not exhaust the meaning of the term *freedom* for the Friends of the Atlantic Community. To "live in the Light," to bring one's life fully under the dominion of the Truth inwardly revealed, was to enjoy a further and paradoxical kind of liberty. It was a freedom to live one's life in perfect obedience to God's law as set down in Christ's Sermon on the Mount. Just as it was possible for Roosevelt and Churchill, in composing the Atlantic Charter, to translate the highest aims of the Atlantic Community into four great freedoms, so we may express the basic Quaker testimonies—simplicity, equality, community, peace—in terms of four inward freedoms: freedom from materialism, from the reliance upon *things*, which deadens the soul; freedom from pride, from an unwarranted sense of superiority, which leads to unjust discrimination among men; freedom from self-centeredness, which denies our interdependence as men; freedom from hatred, which leads to violence and war.

We of the Atlantic Community in the twentieth century are far from having realized these freedoms in our individual or national lives; nor can the Friends themselves, either in their early years or in these latter days, be said to have realized them fully. Yet, whatever their failures in practice, it was given them to glimpse a vision of perfection and, by striving to achieve it within the conditions of their culture, to hold it up as a goal for the Atlantic Community of their day and ours. That is the real historical significance of the Quakers in the civilization of the Atlantic world.

Notes

FOREWORD

1. *Christ and Culture* (New York, 1956), p. 103.

2. *The Atlantic Civilization: Eighteenth-Century Origins* (Ithaca, New York, 1949), p. 58.

3. This—the earliest in date of composition of the pieces printed here—is the only essay which I should develop differently if I were writing it today. The concept of *enthusiasm*, I still believe, accurately describes the religious sensibility of the early Friends, but it can be usefully supplemented by the broader category of *prophetic* as opposed to *mystical* religion. I have discussed this point briefly in my Introduction to the second edition of W. C. Braithwaite's *Second Period of Quakerism* (Cambridge, England, 1960), pp. xxiii–xxiv.

CHAPTER I. *The Atlantic Community of the Early Friends*

1. *The Journal of George Fox*, ed. John L. Nickalls (Cambridge, England, 1952), p. 11.

2. *The Witness of William Penn*, ed. Frederick B. Tolles and E. Gordon Alderfer (New York, 1957), p. 17.

3. For a brief survey of what historians have made of the origins of the movement, see my "1652 in History: Changing Perspectives on the Founding of Quakerism," *Bulletin of Friends Historical Association*, XLI (1952), 12–26.

4. "Natural Religion," in *Uncollected Lectures by Ralph Waldo Emerson*, ed. Clarence Gohdes (New York, 1932), p. 57.

5. *Journal of George Fox*, pp. 103–104.

6. William C. Braithwaite, *The Beginnings of Quakerism*, 2nd ed., revised by Henry J. Cadbury (Cambridge, England, 1955), pp. 86, 551–552.

135

7. Henry J. Cadbury has pointed out that Fox had already foreseen the rise of Quakerism overseas—in Holland, to the eastward, however, rather than in the west. "The Horizon of Fox's Early Visions," *Bull. Friends Hist. Assoc.*, XLVII (1958), 30–34.

8. This generalization must be qualified in one respect. Already, Cromwell was meditating his "Western Design"—the scheme which was to send Admiral Sir William Penn against the Spanish in the West Indies.

9. *The Colonial Period of American History* (New Haven, Conn., 1937), III, ix–xiii.

10. Fulmer Mood, "The English Geographers and the Anglo-American Frontier in the Seventeenth Century," *University of California Publications in Geography*, VI (1944), 373.

11. Estimates of population here and elsewhere are based on contemporary guesses as collected in Evarts B. Greene and Virginia D. Harrington, *American Population Before the Federal Census of 1790* (New York, 1932).

12. George Gardyner, *A Description of the New World: or, America, Islands and Continent* (London, 1651), pp. 45, 92, 93, 96, 100, 101, 103, 104, 160.

13. *The Journal of George Fox*, ed. Norman Penney (Cambridge, England, 1911), II, 338.

14. The names of the first "publishers of Truth" in America are given in an appendix to the first printing of this essay. Supplement No. 24, *Journal of the Friends' Historical Society* (London, 1952), pp. 35–38.

15. Braithwaite, *Beginnings*, p. 319n.; *Letters &c. of Early Friends*, ed. A. R. Barclay (London, 1841), pp. 286–287n.; Isabel Ross, *Margaret Fell: Mother of Quakerism* (London, 1949), Chap. V.

16. John Audland to Margaret Fell, *undated* [1655], James Bowden, *The History of the Society of Friends in America* (London, 1850), I, 42n.; Caton MSS, Library of the Society of Friends, London, III, 427.

17. See Henry J. Cadbury, "Answering That of God," *Jour. Friends' Hist. Soc.*, XXXIX (1947), 9–14.

18. *Journal of George Fox*, ed. Nickalls, p. 263.

19. *The Holy Spirit in Puritan Faith and Experience* (Oxford, 1946), especially pp. 12–14.

20. Since this view of the religious character of the early Virginians is at variance with the conventional "Cavalier" picture, let me cite the observation of the leading student of American Puritanism: "However much Virginia and New England differed in ecclesiastical polities, they were recruited from the same type of Englishmen, pious, hard-working, middle-class, accepting literally and solemnly the tenets of Puritanism . . ."

(Perry Miller, "The Religious Impulse in the Founding of Virginia," *William and Mary Quarterly*, 3rd Ser., V [1948], 501).

21. I am not forgetting that the Puritans of Massachusetts Bay persecuted Friends to the death. But it is an old and true saying that the heretic is more feared than the infidel, the dissident Christian than the atheist or Turk. Compare the attitude—if I may shift my point of reference from *odium theologicum* to *odium politicum*—of the old-line Marxian Socialist toward the Communist, of the orthodox Stalinist toward any sort of "deviationist."

22. See James Fulton Maclear, " 'The Heart of New England Rent': The Mystical Element in Early Puritan History," *Mississippi Valley Historical Review*, XLII (1956), 621–652.

23. If my analysis is correct, two corollaries suggest themselves: (1) that Quaker meetings survived longer in Holland than elsewhere on the Continent because of the quasi-Puritan character of Dutch Protestantism, and (2) that the meetings in the West Indies presently languished and decayed because of the weakness of Puritan influences there.

24. I'have found record of only seven transatlantic visitors between 1663 and 1671.

25. Fox, *Journal*, ed. Penney, II, 168.

26. Frank Bate, *The Declaration of Indulgence*, 1672 (London, 1908), p. 74.

27. *Journal*, ed. Penney, II, 170.

28. William Edmundson, one of the group, preached the first sermon ever heard in North Carolina—to a people "who had little or no Religion, for they came and sat down in the Meeting smoking their pipes" (*A Journal of . . . William Edmundson* [Dublin, 1715], p. 59).

29. See [William Loddington], *Plantation Work the Work of This Generation* (London, 1682).

30. *The Second Period of Quakerism* (London, 1919), pp. 408–409.

31. *Ibid.*, pp. 401–402.

32. This whole subject is treated in greater detail in the essay which follows.

33. *God's Mighty Power Magnified: As Manifested and Revealed in His Faithful Handmaid Joan Vokins* (London, 1691), pp. 31–43.

34. MS. Minutes of Philadelphia Yearly Meeting, Department of Records, Philadelphia Yearly Meeting, Philadelphia, Pa., I, 6.

35. Bowden, I, 60n.; Kirk Brown, "Friends' Libraries in Maryland," *Jour. Friends' Hist. Soc.*, II (1905), 130–131.

36. Braithwaite, *Beginnings*, 319 and note.

37. *Letters &c. of Early Friends*, p. 327.

38. MS. Minutes of Meeting for Sufferings, Library of the Society of Friends, London, I, 65, 71, 73, 74; "Quakers in Barbados," *Jour. Friends' Hist. Soc.*, V (1908), 43.

39. Preface to 1694 *Journal,* sig. I2. Henry Gouldney, in whose house Fox died, confirms Penn's statement. The dying leader, he records, "had a Concerne . . . for the universall good of Friends in all parts and Countreys" (Gouldney to Sir John Rodes, January 15, 1691, *A Quaker Post-Bag,* ed. Mrs. Godfrey Locker-Lampson [London, 1910], p. 52).

40. Thomas E. Drake has begun the study of the later development of the Atlantic Quaker community in his Presidential Address before the Friends' Historical Society, *Patterns of Influence in Anglo-American Quakerism,* Supplement No. 28, *Jour. Friends' Hist. Soc.* (London, 1958).

41. *An Account of the Life of that Ancient Servant of Jesus Christ John Richardson* (London, 1774), pp. 130–131.

42. The effects of the fragmentation of American Quakerism on transatlantic Quaker relations can be studied in the experience of James and Lucretia Mott, who visited England in 1840 on an anti-slavery mission. See *Slavery and "the Woman Question": Lucretia Mott's Diary,* 1840, ed. F. B. Tolles, *Jour. Friends' Hist. Soc.,* Supplement No. 23 (1952). But in *The Anglo-American Connection in the Early Nineteenth Century* (Philadelphia, 1959) Frank Thistlethwaite has incidentally provided much evidence of continuing transatlantic relationships within the Quaker community, especially among businessmen, reformers, and educators.

CHAPTER II. *The Transatlantic Quaker Community in the Seventeenth Century: Its Structure and Functioning*

1. Quoted in Felix Morley, *The Power in the People* (New York, 1949), p. 162.

2. *The Quakers: Their Story and Message* (New York, 1927), Chap. VIII.

3. *Apology for the True Christian Divinity,* Prop. XI, Sec. xvii.

4. *The Works of George Fox* (Philadelphia, 1831), VII, 169.

5. Quoted by Arnold Lloyd, *Quaker Social History, 1669–1738* (London, 1950), p. 5.

6. John Audland to Margaret Fell, 1655, James Bowden, *The History of the Society of Friends in America* (London, 1850), I, 42n.

7. Our knowledge of the Quaker incursions into Surinam and Newfoundland is fragmentary. One John Bowron traveled three or four hundred miles along the lonely stretch of coast between the Amazon and the Orinoco *ca.* 1656, preaching to the natives and attending their worship

"which was performed by beating upon Holly [hollow?] Trees, and making a great noise with Skins, like a sort of Drums" (*Piety Promoted, The Third Part. In a Collection of the Dying Sayings of Many of the People Called Quakers* [Dublin, 1721], p. 248). Of Quaker activity in Newfoundland even less is known. George Fox records that in 1656 "Esther Beedle" (Hester Biddle), a Quaker minister, went thither (*The Journal of George Fox*, ed. Norman Penney [Cambridge, 1911], II, 334). And there is a reference to Quakers on the island three years later in a letter of John Davenport to John Winthrop, September 28, 1659 (Leonard Bacon, *Thirteen Historical Discourses* [New Haven, 1839], p. 378).

8. John Rous to Margaret Fell, September 3, 1658, Swarthmore MSS, Library of the Society of Friends, London (microfilm at Friends Historical Library of Swarthmore College), I, 82.

9. *The Journal of George Fox*, ed. John L. Nickalls (Cambridge, England, 1952), p. 332.

10. For the British Isles see W. C. Braithwaite, *The Second Period of Quakerism* (London, 1921), p. 459; Isabel Grubb, *Quakers in Ireland, 1654–1900* (London, 1927), p. 89. For the American colonies see Rufus M. Jones *et al., The Quakers in the American Colonies* (London, 1911), pp. xv–xvi; Pierre Brodin, *Les Quakers en Amérique au dix-septième siècle et au début du dix-huitième* (Paris, 1935), p. 381.

11. See Barclay, *Apology*, Props. X ("Concerning the Ministry") and XI ("Concerning Worship"); and, for a modern treatment, Howard H. Brinton, *Prophetic Ministry* (Wallingford, Pa., 1950).

12. Rev. John Talbot to the Secretary of the S.P.G., September 1, 1703, *Collections of the Protestant Episcopal Historical Society* (New York, 1851–1853), I, xl–xli.

13. Elizabeth Webb to A. W. Boehm, *ca.* 1711, *Friends' Library*, ed. William Evans and Thomas Evans (Philadelphia, 1837–1850), XIII, 171.

14. *A Journal of the Life, Travels, and Labour of Love in the Work of the Ministry of . . . James Dickinson* (London, 1745), p. 83.

15. I shall use the masculine pronoun henceforward, but it should be remembered that at least a third of the ministers who came to America were women.

16. Bowden, II, 237.

17. Friends along the less-traveled routes did request more visits, however, and some conscious effort was made to supply their needs. From Virginia, for example, came word that meetings were well attended when visiting Friends were present, "but few will com & sett & waight wth us when they are gon"; if the Lord would but send more visitors, the letter continued, Quakerism would wear a more prosperous face in those parts

(Thomas Jordan to George Fox, November 18, 1687, *Jour. Friends' Hist. Soc.*, XXXIII [1936], 57). A similar wish was expressed by John Archdale, a Quaker Proprietor of Carolina (To George Fox, March 25, 1686, *ibid.*, XXXVII [1940], 18). In response to earlier such requests Fox had suggested that "public Friends" in Pennsylvania and New Jersey, where there was a superabundance of ministry, should "divide [themselves] to other meetings, and two and two to visit friends, both in New England, Maryland, Virginia, and Carolina . . ." (To ministering Friends, May 20, 1685, *Pennsylvania Magazine of History and Biography*, XXIX [1905], 105–106).

18. Bowden, I, 39–41, 135–137.

19. *A Collection of Memorials Concerning Divers Deceased Ministers . . . in Pennsylvania, New-Jersey, and Parts Adjacent* (Philadelphia, 1787), pp. 4–5.

20. *A Journal of the Life, Travels, Sufferings, and Labour of Love in the Work of the Ministry of . . . William Edmundson* (Dublin, 1715), pp. lvii, lviii, 52–67, 69–101, 108–112.

21. "Intercolonial Solidarity of American Quakerism," *Pa. Mag. of Hist. and Biog.*, LX (1936), 366.

22. The correspondence of William Ellis is more revealing on this score than that which has survived from any other minister of the period. When he and a companion announced their intention of traveling to America in 1697, a friend asked them to seek out the family of a kinsman in West New Jersey and "take account from them of their welfare, both as to things of this life and to the Truth" (John Tomkins to William Ellis and Aaron Atkinson, December 1, 1697, James Backhouse, *The Life and Correspondence of William and Alice Ellis* [London, 1849], pp. 40–41). In Pennsylvania a Welsh Friend asked him, should he ever visit Dolgelly Meeting in Merionethshire, to inquire for his daughter "if she be then alive, and for her husband who is a priest." "If thou findest thyself free, and anything inclined thereunto," he went on, "knock at his door, and see whether she is quite dead, or slumbering among the dead" (Rowland Ellis to William Ellis, March 28, 1699, *ibid.*, pp. 121–122).

23. "Concerning Our Monthly and Quarterly and Yearly Meetings," *Letters, &c., of Early Friends*, ed. A. R. Barclay (London, 1841), p. 313.

24. See *Jour. Friends' Hist. Soc.*, XXI (1924), 42–43, for the first list of representatives, dated June, 1676.

25. Braithwaite, *Second Period*, p. 267.

26. MS Minutes of the Meeting for Sufferings, Library of the Society of Friends, London (microfilm at Friends Historical Library of Swarthmore College), Vol. I, pp. 2, 3, 5, 23, 39, 40.

27. *Ibid.*, IV, 65, 71, 73, 74; *A Collection of the Epistles from the Yearly Meeting of Friends in London* (Baltimore, 1806), pp. 21–22, 25; [Samuel Tuke], *Account of the Slavery of Friends in the Barbary States* (London, 1848), pp. 17–22; *Jour. Friends' Hist. Soc.*, V (1908), 43; Shippen to William Ellis, September 27, 1699 (Backhouse, *William Ellis*, p. 153).

I have not stressed the business relations between Quaker merchants as a factor in strengthening the transatlantic Quaker community, since that was largely a development of the eighteenth century. See Frederick B. Tolles, *Meeting House and Counting House: The Quaker Merchants of Colonial Philadelphia* (Chapel Hill, 1948), pp. 89–91. But hostile critics were already charging that the Friends and their Society prospered "by keeping their Trade within themselves" (George Keith, *et al.*, "An Account of the State of the Church in North America," *Coll. Prot. Epis. Hist. Soc.*, [New York, 1851–1853], I, xix).

28. *Letters &c., of Early Friends*, pp. 316–317.

29. *Epistles*, I, 159–164. As early as 1656 he had written "A paper to be scattered abroad all over the West Indies," but this was undoubtedly, if I may return to my earlier military metaphor, in the nature of a "propaganda barrage" designed to "soften up" the inhabitants for the missionary offensive which was just beginning. See *Annual Catalogue of George Fox's Papers*, ed. Henry J. Cadbury (Philadelphia, 1939), p. 59.

30. Bowden, I, 355–357, 377–381; Jones *et al.*, pp. 313–314. Even before Fox's death, Maryland Friends were writing to his wife, addressing her as their "dear and tender nursing mother" (Isabel Ross, *Margaret Fell: Mother of Quakerism* [London, 1949], p. 289).

31. I arrive at this figure by adding to those reprinted in his *Works* (vols. VII–VIII) the ones listed in the *Annual Catalogue* of his writings but not reprinted.

32. *Epistles*, I, 144–145; Thomas E. Drake, *Quakers and Slavery in America* (New Haven, 1950), p. 5; Bowden, I, 414; *Epistles*, II, 210–211, 86–92; *Jour. Friends' Hist. Soc.*, V (1908), 101.

33. Not to be overlooked are the epistles written to American meetings by other prominent Quaker leaders. Josiah Coale, for example, wrote to Friends in Holland, Jamaica, New England, and Maryland, and requested that his epistles be "circulated among Friends in these places and read in their meetings" (*The Books and Divers Epistles of Josiah Coale* [(London), 1671], pp. 44–70). Moreover, there was much private correspondence between "public Friends" and members of meetings which they had visited. See the letters written to William Ellis by Pennsylvania Quakers after his return to England, Backhouse, pp. 112–168.

34. *Letters &c., of Early Friends*, p. 315.

35. MS Minutes of Philadelphia Yearly Meeting, Department of Records, Philadelphia Yearly Meeting (microfilm at Friends Historical Library of Swarthmore College), I, 4.

36. Despite the diligent attempts of the New England authorities to confiscate the "Erroneous Books and hellish Pamphlets" which the early Quaker missionaries brought with them, search of a house in Hampton in 1658 uncovered copies of books by William Dewsbury and John Lilburne, both Quakers (Joseph Besse, *A Collection of the Sufferings of the People Called Quakers* [London, 1753], II, 188). In the same year there is an item in the accounts of a fund collected at Kendal "for the service of Truth," indicating that books had been sent to Virginia (Bowden, I, 60n); and the Governor of Jamaica was reporting that Quaker tracts were being distributed in that island (Jones *et al.*, p. 43).

37. Kirk Brown, "Friends' Libraries in Maryland," *Jour. Friends' Hist. Soc.*, II (1905), 130–131; MS Minutes of Philadelphia Yearly Meeting, I, 23–24.

38. See Charles R. Hildeburn, *The Issues of the Press in Pennsylvania, 1685–1784* (Philadelphia, 1885), I, 5, 17, 19–20.

39. George Keith's *Presbyterian and Independent Visible Churches in New England and Elsewhere, Brought to the Test*, written before its author's apostasy from Quakerism, and printed by Bradford in 1689, was reprinted in London in 1691. Jonathan Dickinson's *God's Protecting Providence*, first published in Philadelphia in 1699, was reprinted in London in 1700 and again in 1701; it was to go through at least six editions in England in the eighteenth century. See *Jonathan Dickinson's Journal*, ed. E. W. Andrews and C. M. Andrews (New Haven, 1945), Appendix B, pp. 177–187.

40. The third major schism—that of Wilkinson and Story—arose, like that of Perrot, in England, but was felt as far away as Barbados. See Braithwaite, *Second Period*, pp. 348–349.

41. Bowden, I, 329, 348, 351–353, 371–372; William I. Hull, *Benjamin Furly and Quakerism in Rotterdam* (Swarthmore, Pa., 1941), pp. 228–232.

42. *Epistles*, I, 273–274, 306, 309–310; *The Truth Exalted in the Writings of . . . John Burnyeat* (London, 1691), pp. 32–35, 41–43.

43. A careful account of this movement is found in Ethyn W. Kirby, *George Keith* (New York, 1942), Chaps. V–VII.

44. Hugh Roberts to William Penn, *ca.* 1692, *Pa. Mag. of Hist. and Biog.*, XVIII (1894), 208.

45. MS Minutes of Philadelphia Yearly Meeting, I, 78. The echoes, however, were slow in dying: in 1703 one Francis Bugg tried to revive

Keith's attack on "Foxonian" Quakerism in a broadside with the suggestive title *A Bomb Thrown amongst the Quakers in Norwich, Which Will Reach Their Friends in Bristol, and Set Fire to the Combustible Matter thorow Their Whole Camp in England, Wales, and America.* This blast was promptly reprinted in New York, but so effective were the Quaker fire-prevention measures in America that it fizzled out and utterly failed to start a second conflagration.

46. *Quakers in the American Colonies,* pp. 314–315. Quoted by permission of the Joseph Rowntree Charitable Trust.

CHAPTER III. *Quakerism and Politics*

1. *The Journal of George Fox,* ed. John L. Nickalls (Cambridge, England, 1952), p. 65.

2. See Robert O. Byrd, "Quakerism and Foreign Policy," *Bulletin of Friends Historical Association,* XLVIII (1959), 3–20.

3. To Eliza P. Gurney, September 4, 1864, *The Collected Works of Abraham Lincoln,* ed. Roy P. Basler (New Brunswick, N.J., 1953), VII, 535.

4. *Journal of George Fox,* p. 274.

5. *Ibid.,* pp. 197–198.

6. For the social and political climate of the 1650's see W. Schenk, *The Concern for Social Justice in the Puritan Revolution* (London, 1948).

7. Both this passage and that from William Tomlinson below are taken from a revealing article by James F. Maclear, "Quakerism and the End of the Interregnum: A Chapter in the Domestication of Radical Puritanism," *Church History,* XIX (December, 1950), 240–270.

8. *Journal of George Fox,* pp. 103–104. T. Canby Jones places Fox in relation to the eschatology of his time in "George Fox's Understanding of Last Things," *Friends' Quarterly,* VIII (October, 1954), 194–206.

9. Maclear, *op. cit.,* p. 255.

10. *Letters &c., of Early Friends,* ed. A. R. Barclay (London, 1841), pp. 280–281.

11. *Journal,* p. 358.

12. *Ibid.,* pp. 398–404.

13. *Letters &c., of Early Friends,* p. 368.

14. William C. Braithwaite, *The Second Period of Quakerism* (London, 1919), pp. 90, 98. Ethyn Williams Kirby gives a good account of "The Quakers' Efforts to Secure Civil and Religious Liberty, 1660–96," in the *Journal of Modern History,* VII (1935), 401–421.

15. Kirby, *op. cit.,* 402, 405–406.

16. Fulmer Mood, "William Penn and English Politics in 1680–81," *Journal of the Friends' Historical Society,* XXXII (1935), 3–21.

17. W. C. Braithwaite, *The Beginnings of Quakerism,* 2nd ed., revised by Henry J. Cadbury (Cambridge, England, 1955), pp. 454–455.

18. *The Short Journals and Itinerary Journals of George Fox,* ed. Norman Penney (Cambridge, England, 1925), pp. 190–192, 218.

19. Kirby, *op. cit.,* p. 413.

20. *Ibid.,* p. 416.

21. Samuel Scott, *A Diary of Some Religious Exercises and Experience* (London, 1809), p. 12.

22. *Journal of the Life and Labours of Thomas Shillitoe* (London, 1839), I, 224.

23. Quoted in Rufus M. Jones, *The Later Periods of Quakerism* (London, 1921), II, 633.

24. Margaret E. Hirst, *The Quakers in Peace and War* (London, 1923), pp. 285–87, 288–91.

25. Edwin B. Bronner, "John Bright and the Factory Acts," *Bulletin of Friends Historical Association,* XXXVIII (1949), 92–102.

26. *Extracts from the Minutes and Epistles of the Yearly Meeting . . . Relating to Christian Doctrine, Practice, and Discipline* (London, 1861), pp. 123, 124.

27. *Christian Discipline of the Religious Society of Friends of London Yearly Meeting,* Part II, *Christian Practice* (London, 1911), p. 126.

28. Betty Ann Hershberger, A Pacifist Approach to Civil Government: A Comparison of the Participant Quaker and the Non-Participant Mennonite View (typewritten B.A. thesis, Swarthmore College, 1951).

29. Quaker experience in governing Pennsylvania has been variously evaluated by historians. For a less critical interpretation than mine, see Isaac Sharpless, *A Quaker Experiment in Government* (Philadelphia, 1898); for a more critical view, Daniel J. Boorstin, *The Americans: The Colonial Experience* (New York, 1958), Chaps. 7–11.

30. *The Discipline of Friends, Revised and Approved by the Yearly Meeting, Held at New Garden, in Guilford County, N.C., in the Eleventh Month, 1854* (Greensboro, N.C., 1855), p. 16.

31. This advice appears in the *Rules of Discipline* of Philadelphia Yearly Meeting before the Great Separation, and was retained in both Orthodox and Hicksite Disciplines for a considerable period thereafter.

32. *The Book of Discipline of the Religious Society of Friends* (Philadelphia, 1927), pp. 57–58.

33. *Faith and Practice of the Five Years Meeting of Friends in America* (Richmond, Ind. [1946]), pp. 38–39.

34. *Faith and Practice of the Philadelphia Yearly Meeting of the Religious Society of Friends* (Philadelphia, 1955), p. 42.

35. *Quakers in the American Colonies* (London, 1911), pp. 175–176. Quoted by permission of the Joseph Rowntree Charitable Trust.

36. Quoted in F. W. Sollmann, *Religion and Politics* (Wallingford, Pa., n.d.), pp. 5–6.

37. I have collected some examples of Quakers visiting heads of state in "Friends and the Rulers of the People," *Friends Intelligencer*, CV (July 10, 1948), 391–392.

38. Zechariah 4:6.

CHAPTER IV. *Quakerism, Capitalism, and Science*

1. "Economic Life," *The Quaker Approach to Contemporary Problems*, ed. John Kavanaugh (New York, 1953), p. 51.

2. *Ibid.*, p. 46. A great deal of information about English Quaker businessmen will be found in Arthur Raistrick's *Quakers in Science and Industry* (New York, 1950) and Paul H. Emden's *Quakers in Commerce* (London, 1940), but neither author comes to grips with the nexus between the Quaker ethic and the spirit of business enterprise. Isabel Grubb's *Quakerism and Industry Before 1800* (London, 1930), also limited to the British Isles, reviews both individual and official Quaker pronouncements on business ethics.

3. I have attempted in *Meeting House and Counting House* (Chapel Hill, 1948), Chaps. III–V, to deal with both aspects of the Quaker ethic as reflected in the theory and practice of the colonial Philadelphia Quakers.

4. *Man's Disorder and God's Design: The Amsterdam Assembly Series*, Vol. III: *The Church and the Disorder of Society* (New York, n.d.), p. 195.

5. *The Writings of Benjamin Franklin*, ed. A. H. Smyth (New York, 1905–1907), I, 274–276, 285–286, 289.

6. See Max Weber, *The Protestant Ethic and the Spirit of Capitalism*, trans. Talcott Parsons (New York, 1930), pp. 48 ff. Ernst Troeltsch makes the significant blunder of calling Franklin a Quaker (*The Social Teaching of the Christian Churches*, trans. Olive Wyon [New York, 1931], II, 783).

7. *The Journal of George Fox*, ed. John L. Nickalls (Cambridge, England, 1952), pp. 169–170.

8. [Giovanni Paolo Marana] *Letters Writ by a Turkish Spy* (10th ed., London, 1734), VI, 17.

9. Charles Leslie, *The Snake in the Grass* (London, 1698), p. 362.

10. See, for example, Werner Sombart, *The Quintessence of Capitalism*, trans. M. Epstein (London, 1915), p. 287.

11. *To the Parliament of the Comon-wealth of England* (London, 1659), p. 5.

12. *The Social Ideas of Religious Leaders, 1660–1688* (London, 1940), p. 235.

13. *No Cross, No Crown*, in *The Witness of William Penn*, ed. Frederick B. Tolles and E. Gordon Alderfer (New York, 1957), pp. 47–48.

14. Perry Miller, *The New England Mind* (New York, 1939), p. 42.

15. Israel Pemberton to John Pemberton, June 7, 1749, Pemberton Papers, Historical Society of Pennsylvania, V, 107.

16. *The Works of George Fox* (Philadelphia, 1831), VII, 345.

17. *No Cross, No Crown, loc. cit.*, p. 48.

18. *A Journal, or Historical Account of the Life, Travels, and Christian Experiences, of that Antient, Faithful Servant of Jesus Christ, Thomas Chalkley*, in *A Collection of the Works of Thomas Chalkley* (Philadelphia, 1749), pp. 97–98.

19. *Ibid.*, p. 52.

20. James Logan to John Askew, July 9, 1717, Logan Letter Books, Logan Papers, Historical Society of Pennsylvania, IV, 37.

21. *Journal, Works*, p. 37.

22. Isaac Norris to Joseph Norris, April, 1719, Norris Letter Book, 1716–1730, Norris Papers, Historical Society of Pennsylvania, pp. 183–184.

23. *Autobiography*, in *Writings*, I, 307.

24. The Book of Discipline as Revised by the Yearly Meeting for Pennsylvania and New Jersey in the Year 1719, MS copy in Friends Historical Library of Swarthmore College, pp. 15, 76.

25. *Journal*, ed. Nickalls, p. 169.

26. *The Rise and Progress of the People Called Quakers*, in *The Witness of William Penn*, p. 24.

27. John Reynell to Elias Bland, June 22, 1743, Reynell Letter Book, 1741–1744, Coates-Reynell Papers, Historical Society of Pennsylvania.

28. Jean Pierre Brissot de Warville, *Nouveau voyage dans les Etats-unis de l'Amérique septentrionale* (Paris, 1791), II, 187.

29. *Autobiography, Writings*, I, 328.

30. Abel James to Benjamin Franklin, *ibid.*, I, 313–314.

31. Henry J. Cadbury, "George Fox and the Royal Society," *Bulletin of Friends Historical Association*, XL (1953), 90–91.

32. See A. Ruth Fry, *Quaker Ways* (London, 1933), pp. 214–215.

33. SSRS Newsletter, I (December, 1949), 1.

34. Robert K. Merton, "Science, Technology and Society in Seventeenth Century England," *Osiris*, IV (1938), 465. A summary of Merton's path-breaking treatment of the relationship of Puritanism and science.

with a valuable bibliographical postscript, will be found in his *Social Theory and Social Structure* (2nd ed., Glencoe, Illinois, 1957), Chap. XVIII.

35. Merton, "Science, Technology and Society," *loc. cit.*, p. 452.

36. Irene Parker, *Dissenting Academies in England* (Cambridge, England, 1914).

37. Richard F. Jones, *Ancients and Moderns: A Study of the Background of the Battle of the Books* (St. Louis, 1936), pp. 112–113.

38. *A Serious Apology for the Principles and Practices of the People call'd Quakers*, in *A Collection of the Works of William Penn* (London, 1726), II, 56.

39. *Some Fruits of Solitude*, in *The Witness of William Penn* (New York, 1957), p. 169.

40. *The Early Lectures of Ralph Waldo Emerson*, ed. Stephen E. Whicher and Robert E. Spiller (Cambridge, Mass., 1959), I, 168.

41. *The Rise and Progress of the People Called Quakers*, in *The Witness of William Penn*, pp. 42–43.

42. *Journal*, ed. Nickalls, p. 520.

43. Minute of Six Weeks Meeting, May 11, 1675, quoted in W. C. Braithwaite, *The Second Period of Quakerism* (London, 1919), p. 528.

44. Letter to Sir John Rodes, January 18, 1690, *A Quaker Post-Bag*, ed. Mrs. Godfrey Locker-Lampson (London, 1910), p. 21.

45. This point has been made by Dorothy Stimson, "Puritanism and the New Philosophy in Seventeenth-Century England," *Bulletin of the Institute of the History of Medicine*, III (1935), 321–324.

46. *Apology for the True Christian Divinity*, Prop. XV, Sec. ix.

47. *No Cross, No Crown*, in *The Witness of William Penn*, p. 56.

48. *Apology*, Props. V and VI, Sec. xvi.

49. *Wisdom Justified of Her Children*, in *Works*, II, 473.

50. *The Witness of William Penn*, p. 191.

51. *Some Fruits of Solitude*, *ibid.*, pp. 169–170.

52. See, for example, the twenty-first maxim in *Some Fruits of Solitude*, where, in the manner that was to become classic with Paley, Penn cites examples of the cunning contrivance of the human body as so many reasons why man should "Admire and Adore his good and great God" (*Works*, I, 821–822).

53. *Science and the Modern World* (New York, 1925), p. 5.

54. Henry J. Cadbury, "Penn, Collinson, and the Royal Society," *Bulletin of Friends Historical Association*, XXXVI (1947), 19–24.

55. *Ibid.*, p. 24.

CHAPTER V. *The Quaker Esthetic*

1. *The Witness of William Penn,* ed. Frederick B. Tolles and E. Gordon Alderfer (New York, 1957), pp. 47–48.

2. Perry Miller, *The New England Mind* (New York, 1939), pp. 257–259.

3. *Apology for the True Christian Divinity,* Prop. IV.

4. *Friends for 300 Years* (New York, 1952), Chap. 7.

5. *Ibid.,* p. 135. Quoted by permission of Harper and Brothers.

6. *Some Fruits of Solitude,* in *The Witness of William Penn,* p. 175.

7. Epistle CXI, *The Works of George Fox* (Philadelphia, 1831), VII, 110.

8. Anthony Garvan, "The Protestant Plain Style before 1630," *Journal of the Society of Architectural Historians,* IX (October, 1950), 5–13.

9. *Op. cit.,* p. 12. Cf. Hubert Lidbetter, "Quaker Meeting Houses, 1670–1850," *Architectural Review,* XCIX (1946), 99–116, for a survey of English Quaker architecture.

10. *Some Fruits of Solitude,* in *The Witness of William Penn,* p. 179. The fullest exposition of the early Quaker theory of prose style will be found in Penn's preface to *The Written Gospel-Labours of That Ancient and Faithful Servant of Jesus Christ, John Whitehead* (London, 1704), where Penn warns the reader of Quaker books not to expect "the Learning of the Schools," "a nice or polished Stile," or merely intellectual stimulation. See Luella M. Wright, *The Literary Life of the Early Friends* (New York, 1932), Chap. V; and cf. Jackson I. Cope, "Seventeenth-Century Quaker Style," *PMLA,* LXXI (1956), 725–754.

11. *Memoirs of the Life and Religious Labors of Edward Hicks* (Philadelphia, 1851), p. 71.

12. *A Portraiture of Quakerism* (New York, 1806), I, 66–67. Robert Barclay admitted that the singing of psalms, "when it . . . arises from the divine influence of the Spirit," might be a legitimate part of religious worship, but added that as for "artificial music, either by organs, or other instruments, or voice, we have neither example nor precept for it in the New Testament" (*An Apology for the True Christian Divinity,* Prop. XI, Sec. xxvi).

13. *No Cross, No Crown,* in *The Witness of William Penn,* p. 56.

14. See *The Journal of George Fox,* ed. John L. Nickalls (Cambridge, England, 1952), pp. 169–170.

15. W. C. Braithwaite, *The Beginnings of Quakerism* (2nd ed., Cambridge, England, 1955), p. 519.

16. *A Brief Narrative of the Life of Gilbert Latey,* in *The Friends' Library* (Philadelphia, 1837–1850), I, 172.

17. *Ibid.,* I, 181–182.

18. Epistle CCL, *Works of George Fox,* VII, 300–301; see also Epistle CCCXCVII, *ibid.,* VIII, 256–268.

19. *Apology,* Prop. XV, Sec. vii.

20. *No Cross, No Crown,* in *The Witness of William Penn,* p. 56.

21. Postscript to Epistle from Leinster Province Meeting, in John Rutty, *History of the Rise and Progress of the People Called Quakers in Ireland* (Dublin, 1751), p. 199.

22. W. C. Braithwaite, *The Second Period of Quakerism* (London, 1919), pp. 507–508n.

23. *Some Account of the Life of Joseph Pike,* in *Friends' Library,* II, 379.

24. Sketches of the early Philadelphia meetinghouses and photographs of the Arch Street Meetinghouse are reproduced in Edwin B. Bronner, "Quaker Landmarks in Early Philadelphia," *Historic Philadelphia, Transactions of the American Philosophical Society,* XLIII, Part I (1953), 210–216.

25. Except for Thomas J. Wertenbaker in *The Founding of American Civilization: The Middle Colonies* (New York, 1938), pp. 240–241, historians of American architecture have paid little attention to this highly successful adaptation of form to function in ecclesiastical design. See, however, two articles by F. Charles Thum, a practicing architect: "Balanced Simplicity," *Journal of the American Institute of Architects,* New Series, XIX (1953), 195–200; and "Creative Quaker Architecture," *Friends Intelligencer,* CVII (1950), 587–588.

26. There is a brief discussion of the Quaker journals in my chapter on "Writers of the Middle Colonies" in Robert E. Spiller, et al., *The Literary History of the United States* (New York, 1948), I, 83–86.

27. I restrict myself here to the Philadelphia Quakers, but a study of Quakerism in Newport, Rhode Island, would probably reveal the same tendencies. It is suggestive that the two colonial towns where the cabinetmaker's art reached its peak were both dominated by Quaker influences. The Townsends and Goddards of Newport, who developed the distinctive "blockfront" style of furniture were all Friends, and so were most of their wealthier patrons. See Carl Bridenbaugh, *The Colonial Craftsman* (New York, 1950), pp. 82–84.

28. Frederick B. Tolles, *Meeting House and Counting House: The Quaker Merchants of Colonial Philadelphia* (Chapel Hill, 1948), p. 41.

29. William M. Hornor, *The Blue Book of Philadelphia Furniture* (Philadelphia, 1935), pp. 2–5.

30. MS Epistle dated September 21, 1698, Quaker Collection, Haverford College Library.

31. From our Yearly Meeting Held at Burlington the 20th of 7th mo. 1704: A Generall Testimony Against all Loosness and Vanity or what else may tend to the reproach of Truth . . . , MS in Friends Historical Library of Swarthmore College, pp. 5–6.

32. *The Journal and Essays of John Woolman*, ed. Amelia Mott Gummere (New York, 1922), p. 290.

33. *Ibid.*, p. 267.

34. *Peter Kalm's Travels in North America*, ed. Adolph B. Benson (New York, 1937), II, 652.

35. *Blue Book*, pl. 15, opp. p. 29.

36. Isaac Norris to Joseph Pike, February 25, 1707/8, *Correspondence between William Penn and James Logan*, ed. Edward Armstrong, *Memoirs of the Historical Society of Pennsylvania*, X (1872), 259 (italics mine). Norris may have had in mind the similar argument which Barclay uses with respect to clothing: "We shall not say that all persons are to be clothed alike, because it will perhaps neither suit their bodies nor their estates. And if a man be clothed soberly, and without superfluity, though they may be finer than that which his servant is clothed with, we shall not blame him for it, the abstaining from superfluities, which his condition and education have accustomed him to, may be in him a greater act of mortification than the abstaining from finer clothes in the servant, who was never accustomed to them" (*Apology*, Prop. XV, Sec. vii). The tension between Quaker religious equalitarianism and the conception of a hierarchically ordered society, which the Quaker merchants did not question is discussed in my *Meeting House and Counting House*, pp. 109–113.

37. "The Estate of Jonathan Dickinson," ed. Harrold E. Gillingham, *Pennsylvania Magazine of History and Biography*, LIX (1935), 420–429.

38. "An Early Description of Pennsylvania," ed. Rayner W. Kelsey, *Pa. Mag. of Hist. and Biog.*, XL (1921), 252–253.

39. John Reynell to Daniel Flexney, November 25, 1738, Reynell Letter Book, 1738–1741, Historical Society of Pennsylvania.

40. *Travels*, II, 651.

41. J. P. Brissot de Warville, *New Travels in the United States of America* (London, 1792), pp. 282–283.

42. *A Plea for the Poor*, in *The Journal and Essays of John Woolman*, p. 419.

43. See Tolles, *Meeting House and Counting House*, pp. 234–239.

44. Francis R. Taylor, *Life of William Savery of Philadelphia* (New York, 1925), pp. 428–434; Janet Whitney, *Elizabeth Fry, Quaker Heroine* (Boston, 1937), pp. 42–45, 57–63.

45. I, 69–70.

CHAPTER VI. *Quietism Versus Enthusiasm: The Philadelphia Quakers and the Great Awakening*

1. Aside from the fact that this essay was a by-product of research into eighteenth century Philadelphia Quakerism, there are three good reasons for concentrating on the Philadelphia story. The Quaker City was a focus of revivalistic activity in the 1740's, so that the confrontation was peculiarly direct there. It also happens to have been remarkably well documented. And the parallel story of English Quakerism vis-à-vis the Evangelical Revival has been fully told by Frank Baker in *The Relations Between the Society of Friends and Early Methodism* (London, 1949).

2. *The Writings of Benjamin Franklin*, ed. Albert H. Smyth (New York, 1907), I, 356–357. Franklin's companion was undoubtedly Thomas Hopkinson, first president of the American Philosophical Society. The Quaker defies identification.

3. For a discussion of Quaker quietism see Elbert Russell, *The History of Quakerism* (New York, 1942), pp. 229–240; and, for a more extended treatment, Rufus M. Jones, *The Later Periods of Quakerism* (London, 1921), I, 57–103.

4. *Writings*, I, 355.

5. *Whitefield's Journals*, ed. William Wale (London, n.d.), p. 329.

6. *Journal of George Fox*, ed. John L. Nickalls (Cambridge, England), p. 7.

7. *Whitefield's Journals*, p. 331 (entry for September 30, 1739).

8. *Ibid.*, pp. 337–338 (entry for November 4, 1739). The relationship between the historic and the inward Christ has never been satisfactorily clarified in Quaker thought. For a brief review of the more important Quaker attempts to grapple with the Christological problem, see Edward Grubb's Swarthmore Lecture, *The Historic and Inward Christ* (London, 1914).

9. John Reynell to Daniel Flexney, November 4, 1739, John Reynell Letter Book, 1738–1741, Coates-Reynell Papers, Historical Society of Pennsylvania.

10. Quoted in E. R. Beadle, *The Old and the New, 1743–1876* (Philadelphia, 1876), p. 17.

11. On John Smith see Tolles, "A Literary Quaker: John Smith of

Burlington and Philadelphia," *Pa. Mag. of Hist. and Biog.*, LXV (1941), 300–333.

12. John Smith to John Wardell, April 23, 1740, MS diary of John Smith, Library Company of Philadelphia.

13. Richard Hockley to Bernard Hannington, quoted in *Pa. Mag. of Hist. and Biog.*, XXVII (1903), 322–323.

14. Richard Hockley to Jno. Watson, February 22, 1742, *ibid.*, XXVII, 425–426.

15. *Pennsylvania Gazette*, June 11, 1741.

16. *Whitefield's Journals*, p. 421 (entry for May 12, 1740).

17. The records of Philadelphia Monthly Meeting between the date of Whitefield's arrival and June, 1743, show only five persons dealt with for declining to attend Friends meetings and "joining with other societies in their ways of worship." The minutes are laconic, and one cannot be certain that even these individuals were disowned specifically for consorting with the revivalists.

18. Letter dated May 21, 1740, Smith MSS, Library Company of Philadelphia.

19. Quoted in Beadle, *The Old and the New*, p. 18.

20. *American Weekly Mercury*, July 9–16, 1741.

21. Letter dated July 17, 1741, Pemberton Papers, Historical Society of Pennsylvania, III, 47.

22. Letter dated July 20, 1741, *ibid.*, III, 47.

23. *Apology*, Prop. XI, Sec. viii.

24. *An Account of a Divine Visitation and Blessing, attending the Religious Care and Exercise of the Teachers of Waltham Abbey School* (Philadelphia, 1797), p. 5.

25. MS Journal of Benjamin Ferris, Friends Historical Library of Swarthmore College (entry for October 19, 1741). It was the custom in Friends meetings whenever anyone "appeared in vocal prayer" for all those present to rise, thus showing their unity with the supplicant. By keeping their seats in this instance, the Friends showed their disapproval of the intruder.

26. *Journal of George Fox*, p. 11.

27. *Apology*, Prop. II, Sec. i.

28. *Works* (New York, 1827), I, 176.

29. Quoted by Umphrey Lee in *The Historical Backgrounds of Early Methodist Enthusiasm* (New York, 1931), p. 141.

30. Quoted in Luke Tyerman, *The Life of the Rev. George Whitefield* (London, 1876), I, 220.

31. *Ibid.*, p. 186.

32. Chauncy, *Seasonable Thoughts on the State of Religion in New England* (Boston, 1743), p. 173; Charles H. Maxson, *The Great Awakening in the Middle Colonies* (Chicago, 1920), p. 23.

33. *Whitefield's Journals,* p. 367 (entry for December 12, 1739).

34. *Journal of George Fox,* p. 11; Barclay, *Apology,* Prop. IV.

35. See Jones' Introduction to William C. Braithwaite's *Second Period of Quakerism* (London, 1921), especially pp. xxx–xlv.

36. "I saw that Christ had died for all men, and was a propitiation for all, and enlightened all men and women with his divine and saving light" (*Journal of George Fox,* p. 34). See also Barclay's *Apology,* Prop. V.

37. On perfectionism in Quakerism, see *Journal of George Fox,* pp. 32–33, 56–57; and Barclay's *Apology,* Prop. VIII. For the perfectionism of Wesley see his *Plain Account of Christian Perfection.*

38. *George Fox and the Light Within* (Philadelphia, 1940), Chap. IV.

39. *Apology,* Props. V and VI, Sec. xvi

40. *Works,* VIII, 195.

41. The words of the Duchess of Buckingham, quoted by Lee in *The Historical Backgrounds of Early Methodist Enthusiasm,* p. 129.

42. See George Fox's letter to the Governor of Barbados, *Journal,* pp. 602–604.

43. *A Collection of the Works of William Penn* (London, 1726), II, 781.

44. It is an irony of religious history that within a half-century certain sections of the Society of Friends were to become thoroughly imbued with Evangelical doctrine; this development was to lead to the disastrous separations which rent the Society in the nineteenth century. See Rufus M. Jones, *The Later Periods of Quakerism,* I, 276–287.

45. I borrow here the useful distinction suggested by Umphrey Lee in *Early Methodist Enthusiasm,* p. 16, and worked out in some detail by Joe Lee Davis in "Mystical Versus Enthusiastic Sensibility," *Journal of the History of Ideas,* IV (1943), 301–319. Wesley's antimystical bias is well known.

46. Joe Lee Davis, "Mystical Versus Enthusiastic Sensibility," p. 302.

47. *Ibid.,* 303–304. Quoted by permission of the author and of the editor of the *Journal of the History of Ideas.*

48. *Journal,* p. 11.

49. *The Quaker and Methodist Compared. In an Abstract of George Fox's Journal. With a Copy of His Last Will and Testament, and of the Reverend George Whitefield's Journals. With Historical Notes* (London, 1740), Preface.

50. *Journal and Essays of John Woolman,* ed., Amelia Mott Gummere (New York, 1922), p. 157.

51. Eighteenth century polite literature was full of attacks on enthusiasm. Addison in the 201st *Spectator,* for example, defined it as "a kind of excess of devotion." Many members of the Quaker merchant class were readers of this type of literature, and their attitudes may have been influenced by it.

52. See H. Richard Niebuhr, *The Social Sources of Denominationalism* (New York, 1929), for the best discussion of this process.

CHAPTER VII. *The Culture of Early Pennsylvania*

1. *The Americans: The Colonial Experience* (New York, 1958), pp. 34, 41.

2. *A Further Account of the Province of Pennsylvania,* in *Narratives of Early Pennsylvania, West New Jersey, and Delaware,* ed. Albert Cook Myers (New York, 1912), p. 260.

3. Wesley Frank Craven, *The Legend of the Founding Fathers* (New York, 1956), p. 77. Ellen Starr Brinton gives a brief account of the growth of the legend, with a comprehensive checklist of reproductions of the painting, in "Benjamin West's Painting of Penn's Treaty with the Indians," *Bulletin of Friends Historical Association,* XXX (1941), 99–189. She found approximately seventy-five different prints, not to mention the tablecloths, soup tureens, candle screens, and banknotes on which the scene has appeared as a decorative motif.

4. But *cf.* the remarks of Robert Redfield, a social anthropologist, on the relationship of "high" and "low" culture as parts of "civilization." *Peasant Society and Culture* (Chicago, 1956), pp. 69 *et seq.*

5. Invoice dated February, 1699, Taylor Papers, Historical Society of Pennsylvania, p. 3309. See also Tolles, *Meeting House and Counting House* (Chapel Hill, N.C., 1948), pp. 144–146.

6. So Deborah Norris Logan told John F. Watson, the annalist, on the authority of her mother, Mary Parker Norris, who had grown up in Chester. Watson, *Annals of Philadelphia* . . . (Philadelphia, 1881), I, 129.

7. *Friends for 300 Years* (New York, 1952), p. 184. Quoted by permission of Harper and Brothers.

8. See the estimates of urban population in Carl Bridenbaugh, *Cities in the Wilderness* (New York, 1938), pp. 6, 143, 303, and *Cities in Revolt* (New York, 1955), pp. 5, 217.

9. Manuscript minutes of Philadelphia Yearly Meeting, Department of Records, Philadelphia Yearly Meeting of Friends, I, 54.

10. See above, Chap. V.

11. See, for example, the lament of John Smith, a Chester County Quaker minister, quoted above, p. 85.

12. See Brooke Hindle, "The Quaker Background and Science in Colonial Philadelphia," *Isis*, XLVI (1955), 243–250; also Tolles, *Meeting House and Counting House*, Chaps. 6–9.

13. For Logan's life see Tolles, *James Logan and the Culture of Provincial America* (Boston, 1957). His bibliophilic interests are discussed in Edwin Wolf, 2nd, "The Romance of James Logan's Books," *William and Mary Quarterly*, 3rd Series, XIII (1956), 342–353; his classical scholarship, in Tolles, "Quaker Humanist: James Logan as a Classical Scholar," *Pa. Mag. of Hist. and Biog.*, LXXIX (1955), 415–438; his scientific accomplishments, in Tolles, "Philadelphia's First Scientist: James Logan," *Isis*, XLVII (1956), 20–30.

14. Thus, according to J. Ambler Williams, it was "the more impecunious brethren" among the Welsh who came to Pennsylvania ("The Influence of the Welsh on the History of Pennsylvania," *Pennsylvania History*, X [1943], 120). But Charles H. Browning says they came "of the highest social caste of the landed gentry of Wales" (*Welsh Settlement of Pennsylvania* [Philadelphia, 1912]), p. 27.

15. *The Character of Early Welsh Emigration to the United States* (Cardiff, 1953), p. 13.

16. *Ibid.*, p. 15.

17. Thomas Allen Glenn, *Merion in the Welsh Tract* (Norristown, Pa., 1896), p. 192; Browning, *op. cit.*, p. 525. The story about Edward Foulke is from the manuscript journal of Joseph Foulke, quoted in Howard M. Jenkins, *Historical Collections Relating to Gwynedd* (Philadelphia, 1884), pp. 37–38.

18. *William Penn and the Dutch Quaker Migration to Pennsylvania* (Swarthmore, Pa., 1935). See also "The Dutch Quaker Founders of Germantown," *Bulletin of Friends Historical Association*, XXVII (1938), 83–90, for Dr. Hull's reply to critics who held out for the traditional view that they were German Mennonites.

19. New York, 1950.

20. Princeton, N.J., 1942.

21. See Richard H. Shryock, "The Pennsylvania Germans as Seen by the Historian," in Wood, ed., *Pennsylvania Germans*, pp. 241–249.

22. "A Brief Description of the Province of Pennsylvania, 1753," in Lawrence H. Gipson, *Lewis Evans* (Philadelphia, 1939), pp. 100–101. Richard H. Shryock in his article "British Versus German Traditions in Colonial Agriculture," *Mississippi Valley Historical Review*, XXVI

(1939–1940), 39–54, to which I owe this reference, emphasizes the cultural basis for the superiority of German to English or Scotch-Irish farming practices.

23. Thomas J. Wertenbaker in *The Founding of American Civilization: The Middle Colonies* (New York, 1938), pp. 298–308, stresses the German sources. Harold R. Shurtleff in *The Log Cabin Myth* (Cambridge, Mass., 1939) argues for a Swedish origin. There is no necessary inconsistency here: both Germans and Swedes built log cabins in Europe and could have brought this type of construction to America independently.

24. Wertenbaker, pp. 284–286, 289–290.

25. *Peasant Society and Culture*, p. 140.

26. Logan to John, Thomas, and Richard Penn, April 17, 1731, Penn Manuscripts, Official Correspondence, Historical Society of Pennsylvania, II, 165.

27. Logan to James Steel, November 18, 1729, *ibid.*, 101 (my italics).

28. *We Who Built America* (New York, 1946), p. 61.

29. *Culture on the Moving Frontier* (Bloomington, Ind., 1955), p. 40.

30. Evarts B. Greene and Virginia D. Harrington, *American Population Before the Federal Census of 1790* (New York, 1932), p. 114.

31. *Letters from an American Farmer*, Everyman edition (London, n.d.), pp. 41, 43.

32. Ray A. Billington, "Cultural Contribution versus Cultural Assimilation," in Caroline F. Ware, ed., *The Cultural Approach to History* (New York, 1940), p. 79.

33. "Cultural Groups in the United States," *ibid.*, p. 63. Frederick J. Turner could scarcely have chosen a poorer example than the Pennsylvania Germans to illustrate his thesis that "in the crucible of the frontier the immigrants were Americanized, liberated, and fused into a mixed race . . . " (*The Frontier in American History* [New York, 1946], pp. 22–23).

34. Klees, pp. 417–418, 426–427.

Index

76

5

0